D1237645

SAY YES

A WOMAN'S GUIDE TO ADVANCING HER PROFESSIONAL PURPOSE

TARA JAYE FRANK

GOLD HOUSE PRESS
Books and gifts to evolve the human spirit

© 2015 by Tara Jaye Frank
All rights reserved. Published 2015.
Printed in the United States of America

Design by Erica Keith and Cheryl Viker
Editing by Jacquelyn Fletcher and Karin B. Miller
Author photo by Samuel Jordan Jr.

Gold House Press
P.O. Box 40,
Lakeville, MN 55044
goldhousepress.com

To order in bulk or for wholesale pricing, contact the publisher
at info@goldhousepress.com.

ISBN: 978-1-941933-06-0 (softcover)

≋ DEDICATION ≋

To Eileen Drummond,
who showed me the power of saying yes.

To Lois Hunt, who said yes
to my potential by opening my first big door.

To my husband, John—to whom I would say yes
again and again and again.

TESTIMONIALS

"For any woman who asks how to advance her career or who in the quiet of her own heart wonders whether she can, *Say Yes* is her answer."
> —*Steve Pemberton, Global Chief Diversity Officer, Walgreens Boots Alliance, and Author of* A Chance in the World: An Orphan Boy, a Mysterious Past and How He Found a Place Called Home

"Tara's message is frank, tough, and spot-on for our challenging business climate. She encourages leaders to find their own truth, and gives practical, real-life advice that is highly valuable for both female leaders and their managers. Bravo to *Say Yes* for telling it like it is in corporate America, and for encouraging all of us to unleash the power of women's leadership."
> —*Joan Toth, President and CEO, Network of Executive Women*

"With a keen eye and insight born of experience, Tara Jaye Frank has written a book that does far more than say 'yes' to the leadership potential of women. Her common sense approach and real-life examples chart a compelling course, not only for women and women of color developing their careers, but also for all leaders who have much to gain by being champions of the perspectives and talents women bring to the executive ranks."
> —*Don Hall Jr., President and CEO, Hallmark Cards, Inc.*

"Tara Jaye Frank offers spot-on and inspiring wisdom for women seeking to get ahead in their lives and careers. *Say Yes* is the best guide ever for culturally diverse women. But I can't think of anyone who wouldn't benefit from this practical, clear-eyed guide. Be good to yourself and buy it!"

—*Sally Helgesen, author of The* **Female Vision,** **The Female Advantage,** *and* **The Web of Inclusion**

"Tara's heartfelt blend of personal experience, inspiration, and encouragement makes this book the perfect resource for any woman who aspires to make the leap into leadership. Buy this book for yourself, the women you mentor, and any of the women in your life who deserve to blast through the barriers that stand between them and the leadership roles they're capable of fulfilling."

—*Jo Miller, CEO of Women's Leadership Coaching and Founding Editor of Be Leaderly*

"Every woman who wants to succeed in the business world needs a strategy. This includes when to say yes and when to say no. Tara does a masterful job offering practical tips and insights on how to make the right choices for you. If you want to experience a personal breakthrough that leads to greater success, this book is for you!"

—*Trudy Bourgeois, CEO and founder, The Center for Workforce Excellence, and author of* **Her Corner Office** *and* **The Hybrid Leader**

"Tara is a phenomenal leader with a unique gift for communication. She's incredibly inspiring and tremendously practical—a rare and formidable combination. In these pages, she'll inspire you, equip you, and encourage you to be a better leader so you can fully live out your purpose. This book is a real treat, enjoy!"

—*Susana Eshleman, President and CEO, Children International*

CONTENTS

INTRODUCTION

One of the most inspiring women I ever worked with told me her success secret when I was in my mid-twenties. Her role at Hallmark was one I aspired to, so I was always especially attentive when she offered me wisdom. She was the vice president of creative writing and editorial at the time, and I was an editorial director. When I asked her if she had any general advice for me, she replied simply, "Always say yes." She went on to explain that every time she was asked to do something new, to solve a hairy problem, or to help another person—she said yes. And this straightforward but profound approach to her career had stretched her more than any one isolated experience ever had.

Over the years, I've come to understand the substance behind her response. Always saying yes isn't about doing everything people ask you to do. It's not about sacrificing your personal truth to please others or about bowing down. It's about believing the best in yourself and other people. It's about unbridled optimism—embracing the idea that you have more creative power than you know, and understanding how you can intentionally use it to achieve your goals and do your special brand of good in the world. That is exactly what I want to help you do with this book.

For almost twenty years, I've charted my course as a Black female executive while witnessing many other women attempt the same, some more successfully than others. No one can claim to have the quintessential answer to succeeding as a woman in the business world. Far too many nuances exist in organizations, job types, business challenges, and, quite frankly, in our own preferences and personalities. But some universal truths supersede these differences. There are principles that, if you not only understand them but also embrace them, will increase your chances of achieving your own personal high bar.

> " *A truly successful career is not about ladders or titles. It's about alignment.* "

Succeeding in the business world has as much to do with knowing and committing to yourself as it does with knowing and committing to your work. It takes time and energy to tap into your professional power and to use it authentically. A truly successful career is not about ladders or titles. It's about alignment. And if you are steadfast and flexible, courageous and judicious, tough and kind, thoughtful about the future and present in the now, you can attain heights greater than you ever imagined.

My last job in the creative department was vice president of creative writing and editorial, in which I led a 150-person organization responsible for applying emotional content across all products. I was the first Black female to become vice president at Hallmark. At the time I was promoted to an executive level, I was the youngest female of any ethnicity to have earned such a rank. People have asked me about the secret to my success. There's not a simple answer to that question, and it's not really a secret. My career success has been due to a combination of things, not the least of which is God's grace and a healthy dose of divine intervention. But I will say this: I've come to understand that vision—knowing what I wanted to experience and how I wanted to contribute—played a major role in turning a few dreams into reality. I also attribute my current success to what I've learned from the times I didn't say yes.

Over the course of five years, I worked directly with Dr. Maya Angelou as her editor for a Hallmark product line called Life Mosaic. Toward the end of our working relationship, she told me in clear terms that she wanted to help me and asked that I call her directly should I ever need anything. I never made the call. Because I wasn't clear about how she could help me and didn't want to waste her valuable time, I let the offer go. When she passed away in 2014, I mourned for many reasons. The world lost an advocate for peace and justice. The literary community lost a treasure. Women lost a role model. And I missed the opportunity of a lifetime. I keep her book *Maya Angelou: The Poetry of Living* on my desk as a way of staying connected to her and her wisdom. She played a significant role in the woman and leader I've become.

Three days after she passed away, I wrote a note to myself that reads, "I will not be afraid to walk through any open door." I share this story, which I once considered a personal failure, as a way to encourage you to say yes. Say yes to you. Say yes to opportunity. Say yes to stretch and growth and risk and support, because you never know when one moment of truth will be the springboard for delivering the gifts you alone can bring to the world.

A Love Letter to You from the Business World

Dear (insert your name):

I have a confession to make. I can't live without you. The truth is, something has always been missing, but I'm finally starting to feel the pain of not having you around. There are people I want to help, and I can't help them unless they trust me. They won't trust me until I develop a relationship with them. I can't develop a relationship with them until I really know them. And I don't know them well enough. But you do. You know what they believe, what they like, how they live, what they're motivated by. And, if I have a prayer of giving them what they really value, it's important that I know these things too.

So while I may not have always recognized what you bring to this relationship, I'm telling you now—I can't live without you. I'm ready to commit to being a true partner to you, and I hope you're ready to commit to me. Together, we can make a meaningful difference for a lot of people. I'd like to start today.

Warm regards,
The Business World

If the message in this letter sounds completely foreign to you, and you rolled your eyes through the entire thing because it's *that* out of sync with the way your business behaves, this means your company's leadership is lagging behind the times. Unless they're selling something only non-Hispanic, white, boomer, and silent men want, it's just a matter of time before you start hearing hints of the above message from the mouths of your executive leaders. If you don't, well, the numbers don't bode well for them.

If, however, the message in this letter sounds even vaguely familiar, I offer you my congratulations. Chances are, you work for, or are somehow connected to, one of the many companies that embrace both the cultural value of diversity and inclusion, and the absolute need for it.

Businesses of every size and ilk are coming to know, in tangible ways, that winning in a culturally diverse world requires a depth of insight into segments they've long ignored or marginalized. And as that realization sets in, they're seeing that the most direct route to being a more insightful organization is paved by the people who travel it every day. Not only do they need more women in general and women of color in the ranks, they need them in influential positions. These positions must offer enough clout to facilitate what I call a new mindset creation—a paradigm shift where incumbents stop assuming they know everything about consumers and become curious again. Leaders who have long relied on their intuition may find it lacking in this new American reality. They are not this new consumer. Their focus group of one holds less weight as time goes on.

And that's why they need you. Having you at the table means a greater chance of truly understanding the fastest-growing segments of our population, and of knowing what to do with that enhanced understanding. Having you in a leadership position means that as investments are determined, decisions are made, and policies evolve, cultural influence can be applied. You can help ensure that your company is considering the people you undoubtedly need to engage to grow your business.

Consider the following statistics in research by Catalyst, Corporate Counsel Women of Color, and Farah Ahmad and Sarah Iverson in the recent study "The State of Women of Color in the United States." Women make more than 85 percent of purchasing decisions in the United States. And by 2050, women of color will make up 53 percent of the female population. Hispanic women will lead this growth, increasing from a share of 16.7 percent of the female population in 2015 to 25.7 percent in 2050. The percentage of Asian women will similarly grow by 80 percent to 7.8 percent in 2050, and the percentage of African-American women will grow from 12.8 percent to 13.3 percent during the same time period.

In addition, the share of women who identify with two or more races will grow, increasing from 2.1 percent in 2015 to 4.1 percent in 2050. (I suspect this is low.) White women, however, will drop from 61.8 percent of the female population in 2015 to 47 percent in 2050. All of these numbers tell a story: They say that women in leadership are critical to understanding what consumers want and to solving their evolving needs. They also say that cultural diversity within those ranks is as important as gender diversity. The two goals should not be separated in today's business environment, because as populations converge, they are becoming the same thing.

Ironically, while women of color trend toward majority status and the need to effectively market to them increases, their growth in leadership positions is slowing to stagnant. In 2012, women made up 46.9% of the labor force and comprised 51.5% of management, professional, and related positions. But women of color accounted for just 12.3% of the 51.5%. According to a 2014 study by Working Mother Media Research Institute, when it comes to those who report directly to the CEO, 9% are white women, 9% are multicultural men, and 9% are multicultural women. Do the math and it means 73% are white men.

A new mindset—one that smartly leverages the cultural and gender influencers across groups to meaningfully enrich the whole—gives your company a shot to win with people who truly desire to be understood. And most companies want to win with people who are still brand loyal. These people are more likely to tell others when a brand satisfies them and will spend on solutions that meet their needs. At the risk of being dramatic, since there will be more of such people in the future, this means it gives your company a shot at survival.

As you begin to understand this data, companies all over the country are taking it in as well. If they're among the conscious, they are connecting the dots between this changing reality and their long-term viability. Many companies are trying to hire people just like you. They're consulting with search firms to uncover the hidden pool of diverse talent that will have the right mix of skills, experiences, and competencies to enhance their current workforce and to help them win in today's marketplace.

While demographic shifts might be the impetus for corporate America's urgency, this book isn't about demographics. And it's not about recruiting—or marketing to women and ethnic consumers. It's not even about talent-management practices, though many companies could use a book about that. This book is about you. Because as those companies, including the one you're currently working for, continue to search for women leaders with diverse perspectives to enrich their brands and differentiate them from the competition, I want you to be ready.

So how do you get ready?

After mentoring and coaching many women on ways to advance their careers, I came to believe in arming people with a practical approach to executing any given strategy. Like other worthwhile business endeavors, you need a thoughtful strategy if you desire to expand your influence. In *Say Yes*, I've created a plan to help you discover your core values, devise your plan for advancement, and actualize your professional purpose. *Say Yes* includes personal stories captured from interviews with successful women. They share real-life experiences that transformed their leadership philosophies and propelled them to new career heights. These inspired women also offer straightforward advice for how to become a more purposeful leader.

The following pages don't hold the keys to unlocking every door that has kept women from progressing in the workplace. You won't find the cure to racism or sexism here, or the hammer that will shatter glass ceilings all over the country. The fact that I don't fully address those challenges in this book is in no way meant to minimize them. These barriers are real, and they absolutely play a role in why we feel we have to be twice as good as anyone else to get ahead. But what I really hope you discover is that you have more control over your destiny than you think. And there are steps you can take to increase your chances of having the career experience you desire, including the advancement that may very well be eluding you.

I also understand that advancement does not connote success for everyone. For some of us, making a meaningful impact is of utmost importance. Nurturing others, meeting underserved needs, caring for our families—these are the goals of our hearts *and* minds. However you personally define success, the strategies in the following chapters can help you envision, clarify, and reach that goal.

Lead with Passion

Since I was fourteen years old, I wanted to write greeting cards for Hallmark. I grew up in the dense Cape Verdean community of New Bedford on the southeast coast of Massachusetts, about an hour from Boston. New Bedford is a small city as cities go and, during my childhood, it was not a place people tended to leave. Most of my predecessors and peers went to college up the road in Dartmouth or in Boston or Providence. Many people think it's odd when I tell them I knew I wanted to work at Hallmark from such a young age, but those who knew me then remember how I wrote and doodled on every piece of paper I could find. In fact, my first poem was published in our local newspaper when I was six years old.

> *Fish in the water,*
> *Fish in the pond.*
> *One little fish was just born.*
> *One little fish was flapping its fin,*
> *The other little fish was trying to win.*
> *One little fish was crying,*
> *The other little fish was dying.*
> *One little fish was sleeping,*
> *The other little fish was weeping.*
>
> *Age 6*

While it's not award-winning literature, the fact that I was writing about everything all the time was a sign of things to come. For a young person who loved words and art—and who was described by my loving and pragmatic mother as "dramatic" (which I have since redefined as "emotionally in tune")—wanting to write greeting cards for Hallmark made sense. Hallmark was a place where words and images came together to convey emotion, to touch people's hearts, and to enhance their relationships. What else would I possibly want to do? Where else would I possibly want to go?

Fast forward and I'm sitting in Shakespeare class at Spelman College, a historically Black women's institution in Atlanta, Georgia, and my professor announces that Hallmark representatives would be coming to recruit interns for the first time. As you might guess, I had an out-of-body experience. If this wasn't destiny in action, I didn't know what was.

After class, I sprinted to the career center to offer to be tour guide and lunch host for the recruiters. When they arrived, I put it all on the line. I told them how writing for Hallmark was a childhood dream of mine. I asked myriad questions about what they were looking for, and then I tried my best to convince them that I was indeed that *something*. I'm sure I was annoying, but they suffered me patiently and were kind enough to bring back news of my enthusiasm. I won an internship at Hallmark that year, and, after a successful summer, I was offered a full-time job the August of my senior year.

And so, as destiny would have it, I began my professional journey in Hallmark Cards' creative division as a greeting-card writer. To this day, when I tell people I work for Hallmark, they ask if I write greetings cards. Answering that I used to always begins the most interesting conversations. During my time at Hallmark, I have worked on numerous products, met amazing people, and had the privilege of leading some of the brightest and most committed employees I'm convinced I will ever know. The people I've worked with have inspired me to expand my leadership impact.

I hope this book inspires you to do the same.

As my former boss Teri Ann used to say, I hope it makes you interrogate your reality—look in the mirror and see something new and invigorating there.

I also hope you can use the tools I've already shared with countless women—of all ethnicities—to become the best professional you possible. I believe you can realize your full potential by learning how to craft a vision for your future, getting clear about your unique value, and understanding how saying yes to open doors can dramatically change not only your work life but your personal life as well.

Because I am a woman of color, some of the content in this book takes into consideration the unique challenges women of color face and the thought patterns that have at times held us back. But these strategies work for all women, and the stories told in these pages are about women from diverse ethnic backgrounds, life experiences, and industries.

Ultimately, if you're a woman and you want to advance your professional purpose, this book is for you, about you, and because of you. And while it won't singlehandedly change corporate America, it may very well change how you experience it.

SAY YES
TO
PURPOSE

A wise executive coach I know starts every personal-effectiveness session by asking about purpose. She doesn't ask about business purpose—objectives, revenue goals, or ROI. She asks about personal purpose: Why are you here? What do you personally hope to achieve? To give? To change? To become?

These are powerful questions. If we can answer them truthfully, they not only provide clarity, but they remind us that life and work are not wholly distinct from each other. We are human beings first and

"Knowing our purpose keeps us focused on what matters. And when challenges come—which they will—purpose gives us a reason to get up in the morning."

employees second. And we each have an intrinsic motivation that guides our thinking, our behaviors, and, ultimately, our results. Knowing our purpose keeps us focused on what matters. And when challenges come—which they will—purpose gives us a reason to get up in the morning.

1

Uncover Your Beliefs and Values

Your true professional purpose is rooted in your beliefs and values. Many don't give this much thought in a business context, but if you want to maximize your potential and optimize your energy, it's critical to understand your beliefs and values. Most women are naturally empathetic and prefer harmony. When your inner self and the work you do are in harmony, balance and order are created. Without that harmony, you tend to feel off kilter and you may not even be able to articulate why.

I'm sure you've heard countless examples of women who've experienced physical and emotional stress, because they're working against their values. Raquel Eatmon's story is a prime example of what can happen when you're not in sync with your true nature, and it provides inspiration to follow a path toward reconciliation.

Follow Your Internal Compass

Television news is not an easy business to break into. Raquel Eatmon pushed hard to claim her spot in what can be a competitive, demanding, and somewhat surreal field.

Since her early twenties, she had a strong feeling she could excel in news. She was a curious, clear and compelling communicator, and she had a talent for relating to others in a way that made them open up to her, leading to great interviews and memorable stories.

Raquel came from a humble background and was no stranger to struggle. She had witnessed poverty and its associated ills firsthand, and she was troubled by the lack of attention paid to the needs of her community, which was made up of many people of color who lived with little means. The absence of stories about what she deemed meaningful troubled her, and she was enthused about the chance to give her community a voice.

However, on the first day that Raquel stepped into a newsroom, she got the distinct feeling that she did not belong there. She wasn't sure if the source of her uneasiness was fear, self-doubt, or intuition issuing a warning. Whatever the reason, after years of working tirelessly to get into television news, the low hum of discontent devastated her. While she couldn't point to one discreet factor that made her feel this way, she knew several issues were at play. The station's process of chasing down content felt inauthentic to Raquel. What's more, she wasn't free to share news that edified people, because the horrible news of the day always pushed out human-interest stories. A story about young girls from a troubled neighborhood being trained by NASA engineers would fall behind the weather if someone happened to stick up a chicken joint for twenty bucks.

According to Raquel, college doesn't prepare you for the politics of news. She had a long talk with herself about the chasm between her expectations and her experience. She felt stuck, but she resigned herself to the news game, and shifted her energy toward refining her skills. She studied tapes of other news shows on networks like CNN and tried to duplicate their storytelling skills. She practiced her approach, her sound, her engagement tactics. As she honed her skills, larger talent agencies paid more attention to her. Raquel was getting traction, which gave her a sliver of hope that with more prominence might come more influence. Maybe, she thought, she could have a voice in the kinds of stories she would tell.

Eventually, Raquel moved from market No. 58 in Ohio to market No. 5 in Dallas to work for a CBS station. Raquel's family was so proud of her. She was newly married, had started a new job, had moved to a new city—her life was full of fresh beginnings. But no one knew her secret: She despised the work. After work, she'd return home and feel dirty. She sensed her own disingenuousness. Like experiences before and those to follow, sometimes her stories, evenly told, would be edited by a producer or manager and become salacious. Although Raquel felt disconnected from her values, she was making great money. Her dual life was made easy financially—and made painful because of her values' misalignment.

Raquel now thinks of the years she spent in Dallas as her self-discovery era. A news director, who really believed in her, hired her. And because he was such a fan, she worked harder to make him proud instead of sharing her frustrations with him. In time, she began to reclaim the voice she had lost. She finally got clear about what she wanted to do and not do, where she wanted to go and not go. This was good and bad. Raquel's newfound courage was causing problems for her in the workplace. Her boundaries were now well defined, but as she fought for herself, her job situation grew worse.

The strong resistance from those with whom she worked made her return to what felt safe—the standard approach to TV news. But Raquel felt more divided than ever. On camera she was one person. At home, she was someone else entirely. Although she knew this was unhealthy, she kept putting one foot in front of the other. It would have been easier for Raquel if she'd confided in someone, anyone. Instead, she kept her unrest to herself.

In 2008, Raquel connected with a fantastic agent who found her a main anchor position in Alabama. While it was a step down in market size, it was a step up in position and pay. Perfect, right? Wrong. Everything within her said, "Do not take this job." But Raquel didn't listen and packed all of her belongings. With moving day just around the corner, she lost her voice. She thought she was coming down with the flu, but the doctor said Raquel was experiencing no flu: She was actually three days away from having a heart attack. He asked what was going on with her and when she told him, he advised her to stay put. "You need to be still," he said. "What is he talking about?" Raquel thought. "I'm healthy. I work out five days a week." She ignored not only the doctor's orders but her own spiritual prompting.

Raquel's first week as an anchor in Alabama was spent with, as she calls him, "one of the worst human beings" she'd ever met. During the breaks, her co-anchor would curse the camera crew. Her manager would call her between breaks and tell her to part her hair on the same side as it was parted on the billboard, or admonish her pronunciation of "a" or "the." She describes the environment as a pit from hell.

On camera, everything was great. Off camera, she was miserable. Still, she continued to push through, even as the situation grew more complex. Raquel's husband was preparing to move to Alabama, and she tried to convince him that it wasn't a good idea. Meanwhile, the station was marketing its "new girl," putting Raquel on billboards all over the city. The public relations train had started down the track, and just when she thought things couldn't get worse, they did.

In years past, three longtime, white female anchors successively filled the anchor position Raquel now held. When the station publicized their "new girl," they focused on her looks, not her experience or talent. In that southern town, there were people who weren't too happy about the new Black woman in the anchor spot, and Raquel began receiving death threats. She had to travel with an armed guard twenty-four hours a day for an entire month. Many people in that town didn't feel that Raquel was one of them. And they were right.

Three months into the job, as Raquel sat in her dressing room putting on makeup, she started crying and couldn't stop. Then came the chest pains. Without talking to a soul, she marched upstairs and told her general manager she was done. "You can't be done," he said and proceeded to announce how much money they'd spent to promote her. She invited him to sue her, finished the week, and left. Raquel felt instant relief and went home to Ohio.

Some of her family members were disappointed. It made them proud to know she was doing so well and had escaped her humble beginnings. Previously, her mother and grandmother would receive calls from people who saw her at the news desk. Her husband was proud, because he knew how hard she had worked to get into the business— and now she was a successful anchor. But no one understood that she was breaking inside. Raquel was beaten down. She decided to take a break, reboot, and maybe get back into the business.

While on hiatus, Raquel pitched an idea for a women's franchise news segment. "If I can just pour myself into this and do the other work too, it will create the balance I need," she rationalized. She was trying to sell a creative solution to her conflict, but no one was buying. Two months into her sabbatical, she facilitated a gathering that would transform her life.

Raquel planned an elegant evening at her mother's house for sixteen women, ages sixteen to ninety-two, who had positively affected her. She called it "For the Love of My Soul." She hired a violinist and hostesses (girls from the neighborhood), and she served champagne. It was Raquel's way of saying thank you.

In that safe space, she broke into tears as she finally shared what she'd been going through. They were shocked and saddened that they had missed an opportunity to support her. The women began telling their own stories, and as their truths fell out of their mouths, the barriers fell away. The women concluded the evening with a prayer circle, each one having her turn in the center. No one wanted to leave, and one evening turned into three days. It was magical for Raquel and the other participants. She wondered how she could use this format to help transform not only herself but any woman who desired the same level of support and healing she had experienced.

It was around this time that Raquel's decision to walk away from her six-figure salary became real. The recession was in full swing, and Raquel felt like a rag doll in the midst of it. Not only was her paycheck gone, but her husband's hours had been cut in half. They were forced to downsize into a much smaller home, which was almost an hour from her hometown. She sold her car, not because she couldn't make payments, but because she and her husband couldn't afford the upkeep. Facials and manicures became treats of the past. Everything Raquel had been hiding behind—the house, car, makeup, pampering—was taken away. One day she woke up and realized that she had just twenty-eight dollars in her bank account. She and her husband lived on what he made, so as the breadwinner, he kept his car, and Raquel went without. Bit by bit, her successful, comfortable life came apart at the seams. Still, she had a strange objective awareness of what was happening, and she knew she would be okay.

Raquel set out to find a job, but her extensive experience and credentials worked against her. She was perceived as a flight risk. Hiring managers doubted a woman with her résumé would stay in a lesser job due to her professional media background and previous positions. She was repeatedly turned away. This experience only strengthened Raquel's resolve to invest in her personal development. She aggressively pursued seminars and forums, establishing a networking springboard from which she would eventually get back in the game.

One day, while sipping hot tea in her small apartment, Raquel thought, "My God, how did I get here?" She reflected on her childhood, when scarcity was the norm. Somehow she'd found herself right back in that position. She started connecting dots. Did I cause this myself? Why did I work against my instincts? Gradually, the answers came. Raquel realized—in that space of ruins—that having her material possessions stripped away and her persona undone was the best thing that could have happened to her. If she weren't the Mercedes, the brightly colored jackets, the girl on the billboard, then who was she? She was finally forced to figure it out. Looking back, Raquel can see how her trials set the stage for triumph.

Raquel was intent on making something more of her "For the Love of My Soul" experience. She started writing a weekly column, "Be Inspired with Raquel," in a Gannett newspaper, which she still writes today. The column served as an outlet to express her true self and validated her as a writer and motivator. In that column, she announced she was holding a two-and-a-half-hour conference at a local hotel. Twenty-five women registered, and she charged twelve dollars apiece. (She admits she had no idea what she was doing!) She called her conference Woman of Power, and she taught the leadership lessons she had learned throughout her career.

When she was ready to expand, she invited ten women she greatly respected to her home for a meeting of the minds, expecting only half of them to show. Every single one attended. Raquel shared her vision, expressing her hope to create a space for women to be themselves and connect with each other. In true sisterly fashion, they collectively devised a plan and mandated that she execute it by the end of the year.

In her first true attempt at hosting a conference, two-hundred-and-fifty women and a few men attended. Propelled by both inspiration and struggle, Raquel managed the project herself, hustling to attract sponsors, fantastic speakers, attendees, and so on. The second Woman of Power conference in 2014 attracted more than three hundred emerging and executive leaders, fifteen speakers, and almost twenty corporate sponsors. She also wrote and published a memoir of her journey, *Strut Your Stuff: Principles in Purpose, Power, and Position.*

Now Raquel Eatmon is CEO of Rising Media, working on her second book, still writing her column, and annually running the Woman of Power Leadership and Networking Conference. She lives with her husband in a condo near Cleveland, and she says her dream is coming full circle. Having been through the ringer, Raquel says her joy is amplified. She describes her current state as "continued personal and professional development." Her advice? "Open yourself up. Tear down the walls of defensiveness. Live genuinely. And as for the gift of your experience? Always give it away."

Raquel knew her beliefs and values at the start of her career. It was those very values that drew her to news as a platform in the first place. She desired to shine a light on the needs of her community members and edify their human experience in a way she hadn't seen. But as she got deeper into news, she recognized the disconnect between her aspiration and her opportunity. This example isn't a dig at media as an industry. It's actually not about media at all. It's about Raquel and the fact that she was out of alignment with her foundation. The news didn't cause her pain. The disconnect did.

Know What Matters Most

Do you know your beliefs and values? If so, how did you discover them? If not, have you ever thought about them? Defining your purpose starts with knowing what you believe about yourself, your gifts, and your unique role in the world. Your purpose also connects strongly to what you value most as a woman, an employee, and a human being. We are all driven by a sense of self that goes deeper and lasts longer than our weekly or even yearly to-do lists. I've had "purpose" seeds rolling around in me for the better part of ten years. Sometimes these seeds sprout right away. Other times they lie dormant, waiting for the right time or opportunity to burst forth. Our job is to discover more about the soil in which these seeds are planted. Who are we at our core? And what bearing does our value system have on how we shape our professional lives?

In several ice-breaking conversations, I've been asked, "What would you be doing if you weren't doing [whatever job I have at the time]?" My specific answers have changed over the years. But they all amount to the same thing: helping people see the best in themselves and others so they can achieve their own personal high bars. I value people, dreams, and results. I believe everyone has inherent value, and each of us is endowed with unique gifts. It's this foundational belief that makes my current work in multicultural strategy so energizing. Essentially, Hallmark is harnessing the uniqueness associated with culture, gender, family dynamics, and sexual orientation to inform its enterprise-wide efforts. There is so much richness to be gained by knowing and leveraging what is germane to people—from all backgrounds—and raising the game with that insight as the basis for growth. I also believe our individual business success journeys—just like our personal ones—must be inspired and practical at the same time.

These are the beliefs and values that have shaped my leadership development approach. They are "the soil" in which this book—my seed—is planted. No one is perfect. But each of us has a spark that makes us special, and I've never felt so useful as when I've had the privilege of illuminating that spark for another person. I've mentored and coached nearly fifty people in my almost twenty years at Hallmark. The longest-standing relationship is still going strong and was cultivated more than 10 years ago. I've developed a reputation for coaching—not because I'm the most experienced or the best—but because I always say yes, and because I coach the *person*, not the employee. I'm also honest, and people who want to get better know that the truth matters.

Additionally, I've come to understand that when I'm focused on bringing out the best in others, I'm actually doing God's work. I believe we are all given spiritual gifts. The gift of personal insight is one I've cultivated over time and have certainly used to elevate my own professional experience. But honestly, the longer I do this, the more sure I am that it matters most when our gifts are put to work beyond our own wants and needs.

I have a friend I've coached for three years. She and I had a conversation not long ago during which she expressed that it was time for me to take my leadership development approach to the masses. This is not the first time I've heard this message. It's been told to me several times, and I've felt the prompting in my own spirit during my quiet moments with God. But I hadn't yet carved out the time and space beyond my other responsibilities to do anything about it.

This friend not only challenged me—she followed up with names of people who could help me build a bridge from idea to reality. She was my catalyst. She was the force of energy I needed to take everything I inherently know and feel and make it go. All of us need a catalyst to make the moves we know we ought to make but, for whatever reason, haven't. I hope this book is yours.

Your Turn

It's time to write down your beliefs and values. Whether or not you realize it, much of how you move through the world comes from these. Without knowing and committing to your beliefs and values, it's easy to get off course. It's best to be conscious of them. They're the soil in which you plant your professional purpose.

Uncover Your Beliefs:
What do you believe about leadership?

What does it look like? What does it create?
Who does it influence or change?

What do you believe about yourself, relative to that definition?

Who are the leaders you trust? Why? What are the characteristics that define them?

I believe leadership is_____.

I believe I (can/should/am) _____.

Uncover Your Values:

What are your priorities? What do you value most?

The answers may not have the same weight. Family, integrity, collaboration, financial freedom—these are all valid responses, even though they are categorically different.

List them here:

For what in your sphere of influence would you gladly extend yourself?

Of all that you value, if you could only keep three priorities, which would you fight to preserve? How about two? One?

I most value_____.

(List no more than three. But circle the one.)

Hold your values close to you, and don't let go without a conscious, empowered choice to do so.

2

Find Clarity

$\mathcal{L}$earning to succinctly communicate your purpose to others is
an important component of guiding your career in the direction you
truly want to go. Without a purpose clarified by you, you're subject to
others' ideas about you, their stories about you, their inspirations for
you, and their purposes for you. It's true: We all get something from
others—our careers are a culmination of the lessons we've learned and
the relationships from which we've become smarter, stronger, more
experienced. But this purpose thing? That has got to come from you.
And if you ensure it's rooted in your core beliefs and values, you can be
confident that what grows will be the fruit you intended to bear.

I've known many women over the years asked to take on roles or
assignments that didn't necessarily excite them, but that others believed
were squarely in line with their strengths. Tanya is one of these women.
She loves strategy but was seen by leaders as a process expert. Time and

again, she was placed on process-oriented projects, and while she was glad to be sought out, the fact that her reputation was tied to process frustrated her.

I understood why. Tanya is a big-picture thinker. She has a strategic mind and an innate ability to imagine a future based on long-term trends and untapped insights. Her rigor, however, and her gift for structuring and executing plans happened to be what most leaders knew about her. Without a clear declaration about her strategic agility and interests, she continued to be defined by other people's perceptions. Eventually, she clearly communicated her passion for strategy and found her way back to what she loved.

It's one thing to show your commitment to meet the company's needs. It's another to be pigeonholed into projects that continually drain you because of others' ideas of who you are. As Tanya learned, the onus is on you to define your purpose and guide your career with clear intentions.

Your Turn

So, once you've identified the beliefs and values at the root of your professional purpose, how do you communicate those? How do you describe your purpose in words that people will both understand and be inspired by? How will they know, from a mere statement, what you're offering and to whom you're offering it?

To begin, you can start by naming how you actually want to contribute.

Do you want to help? Teach? Build? Change? Fix? Inspire?

Who are you doing it for?

Your family? Your children? Yourself? Your community? Your employees? Your company? Your consumers?

What tangible value do you intend to add to the world?

Help do what? Teach what? Build what? Change what? Inspire toward what end?

It's important to remember that even the most altruistic professional purposes can be accomplished within diverse work environments.

If I told you I wanted to help children express themselves through creativity, you might assume I would have to do that in the educational system or as a member of a nonprofit board. But the people who work at Hallmark-owned Crayola, whose purpose is to champion creatively alive children, do it every day. With their innovative ideas, campaigns to help fund creative arts within schools, products donated to students far and wide, and creative exploration enabled within their retail outlets, they are fulfilling their purpose. Whether they work in research and development, marketing or customer service, they play a role in childhood creativity.

So what's your purpose? Don't just skip ahead. Truly think this through and fill in the blanks. You may end up tweaking your response later, but answer this the best way you can today.

I want to _____

for _____ by _____.

Don't worry. We have more discoveries ahead of us. You have to start somewhere, and getting your thoughts from your head to the page is a must. I used to be surprised by how many professionals with career aspirations beyond their current positions haven't captured this information in writing, but it doesn't surprise me anymore. I know many of us hold these thoughts in our heads and could articulate them well enough if asked. But it's hard to build on thoughts you don't say out loud. And building on is exactly what this book was written to help you do.

3

Align with Your Purpose

Once you've articulated your purpose, how do you make it matter? It's not enough to know what you're here to do. You want to do what you're here to do, yes?

There's a direct connection between our strengths, our passions, and our self-generative energy. When we're engaged in acts that come naturally to us, we are taxed far less. If we're really lucky, sometimes we forget we're working at all.

Your Turn

Now it's time for you to add dimension to your purpose—and to translate it into action. Start by simply asking yourself a series of questions:

- What does your purpose suggest you must think, know, and do in order to live it authentically?

- What does someone with your distinct purpose think about business? Teams? Finances? Partnership? Growth? Communities? Leadership?

- What must you know in order to live your purpose?

• What insights and information must you acquire to be credible?

Here are a few more: If you were living your purpose, what kinds of activities would you engage in? What would you give freely to others versus charge for? If you were given three extra hours in a day, how would you spend your time?

Ever notice that people who demonstrate a true passion for something during their working years end up volunteering in a similar space when they retire? Like a teacher who volunteers reading to kids. Or a doctor who signs up for the Peace Corps.

If there's something you would do for free, there's a good chance your purpose is connected to it. It's what the universe has gifted you for—and there's a self-generating energy associated with our gifts that makes the work easier to do.

Now try completing the three statements below. To fulfill my purpose:

I will think:

I must know:

I will do:

4

Tap into Your Higher Power

Our work is often about more than just work. I believe this is true for women especially. And this is truer as we get older—our work becomes increasingly about making a genuine difference. Whether that desire is rooted in spirituality, our hopes for our children, or a general respect for humanity, we often see things happening on two levels: the one right in front of our faces and the higher one, however we define it.

Whenever people ask me what's kept me at Hallmark for so long, I tell them it's partially due to our company's mission, which is to "make a genuine difference in every life, every day." What's not to like about that?

Are you conscious of a bigger purpose at work in your life? Do you have moments when a problem seems to have a logical answer, and still you're drawn to go another direction? Sometimes our inner voice speaks to us in a whisper, and sometimes it's an all-out holler. There are many ways to learn to connect with your higher purpose. One is to watch for examples of how other people live and learn, and see what resonates with you.

Make the Impossible Inevitable

When I think of professional purpose, I think of my friend Susana. We first got to know each other when she was working for me as part of a culture-changing effort at Hallmark. I found her courageous, talented, and insightful. In no time, she became much more than a colleague. She became my friend.

Susana is patient, kind, and a great listener. She's also a living example of God's love. I often wonder how she does it—operating in love so consistently and confidently. Over the years, she's challenged me to be more giving and forgiving, and to do so without expectation. I struggle at times to live up to this high bar, but I always feel encouraged by her prompting.

Susana learned that in the first third of your life, you learn; the second, you earn; and the last, you give. But one day, while on a run with her mother, she realized she was ready to give a little ahead of schedule.

Susana has a deep and abiding passion for children. She believes that every child should have a chance to live out their full potential, and she finds it unacceptable that the latitude on which many children are born determines their opportunities—or lack of them. There are two groups of children who are especially important to her. One is her own, and the other is the children of the world who are considered the least and the last.

In the business world, risk and reward travel hand in hand. A high-risk business is thought to have the highest possible reward. The opposite is also true. But with children, Susana thought, there is very little risk and immeasurable reward. She knew in her heart that helping children would be the focus of her giving.

Only three days after her enlightening run, Susana received a call from a headhunter. He was searching for a board member for Children International, the largest nonprofit in Kansas City. They wanted a Hispanic female with a marketing background to round out the current board's expertise. Seven of the eleven countries served by the organization are Spanish-speaking countries. Susana is a native Spanish speaker, obviously female, and was working in marketing. Check, check, and check.

After her third round of interviews, the CEO asked Susana to join the board. They had screened nine amazing candidates, but she, they explained, had the most passion. And so, Susana began the first of what would become three consecutive three-year board assignments.

Children International has 220 employees at their international headquarters in Kansas City, about 1,500 employees worldwide, and more than 8,000 volunteers who serve 335,000 children and their families globally. Susana was delighted to be giving her time and energy to a cause she deeply believed in, but she also really enjoyed the work.

Being many years younger than the other board members was a humbling and enriching experience for her, and she learned a tremendous amount from the people with whom she served. She learned to establish herself among the crowd, ensuring that her contributions were credible and her ideas were well formed. She had the benefit of watching accomplished people work through difficult decisions. One board member who owned his own company said something to her that really stuck: "When you don't know what decision to make, don't make any decisions." Simple, but profound bits of truth were par for the course during Susana's years as a board member for Children International.

When Susana first told me this story, she was still serving on the board. Not even three weeks later, she was asked by the board to become the next president and CEO of Children International. I honestly can't say I was surprised. I've known few women who live their faith so completely and who truly strive to be like the God they serve in every encounter, with every person, every time. She is a natural-born leader who follows her heart and collaboratively brings people along, so they, too, feel the spiritual gravity of her vision.

Susana's life is a testament to the fact that when you really care about making a difference, doors open for you to do so. Working on behalf of children is a source of true joy for her. She often talks about how crazy it makes her when people say, "I can't change the world." In her mind, when faced with a challenge of biblical proportions, one can either retreat in fear, or respond with boldness and courage.

Ten years after that fateful run, Susana says she heard a word from God: "When love is the motivation, there are powerful forces at work that make the impossible become the inevitable." Almost one year later, she was presented with becoming CEO of Children International, a challenge of biblical proportions. She chose to respond with boldness and courage, and I believe as surely as I've ever believed anything that hundreds of thousands—maybe someday, millions—of children will be better for it.

Lead with Love

Susana's strong faith is often a light in the darkness for me. We hear leadership experts and faith leaders frequently say, "Associate with people who are where you want to be." I consider myself a woman of faith, but Susana lives hers on a level to which I still aspire. She appeals to the higher being in me. One thing she always talked about when we worked together was the power of love. She suggested books to read, wrote down scriptures for me, and would often share a word she received while praying for me. She firmly believes that love is the greatest gift we can give each other, and that it's most important to love others when they're at their most unlovable.

At the time, Susana's advice was personal in nature, but I've thought a lot since then about the power of love in the work environment. It may sound unorthodox, but I believe we can lead with love. Regardless of how our religious affiliations differ, love is an empowering tool. And just in case this all sounds too ethereal right now, I've captured a few practical applications, inspired by the Bible.

- **Love is patient.** Loving leaders create an atmosphere of calm even as they encourage urgency and demand results. They actively listen, and they leave space for talent and ideas to emerge, knowing that some of the best things in life (and work) take time to develop.

- **Love is kind.** Loving leaders offer praise freely. Generous praise, when well deserved, breeds confident, engaged leaders who know they're making a difference. And making a difference is consistently cited as a top motivation for success.

- **Love does not boast and it is not proud.** Loving leaders care more about doing great work than getting credit for it. Credit-conscious leaders can be productive, but they seldom inspire people to follow. Without inspiration, productivity has limits.

- **Love is not self-seeking.** Loving leaders help employees grow stronger and companies get better results. I recently read an article called "The Core Beliefs of Incredibly Successful People" by Jeff Haden. One belief says, "I'm not self-serving. I'm a servant." I love that idea.

- **Love is not easily angered and it keeps no record of wrongs.** Loving leaders can have high expectations and hold people accountable without instilling fear in their teams. Beware of a leader described as "difficult to work for but gets it done." The best leaders know how to balance business requirements with human ones.

- **Love does not delight in evil but rejoices with the truth.** Loving leaders have integrity. Leadership expert Brian Tracy names integrity as one of seven leadership qualities that stand out from the rest, and he defines the core of integrity as truthfulness. "Integrity requires that you always tell the truth, to all people, in every situation," he says. "Truthfulness is the foundation quality of the trust that is necessary for the success of any business." Amen, Mr. Tracy.

- **Love always protects, always trusts, always hopes, always perseveres.** Finally, loving leaders are trusting and trustworthy. Trust is a key component to collaboration, and a precursor to risk tolerance. Loving leaders create safe spaces for learning. In this fast-paced business environment, continuous learning is essential.

I don't believe any of us is here to serve only our own interests. We may not call it the same thing, but most human beings strive toward something greater than themselves. We want to make a positive impact on society—an impact that ripples outward and onward, and, ultimately, one that allows us to leave the world a little better than we found it. Your purpose is seeded in your beliefs, values, and faith. When you connect to all three, you create a career experience that continually expands to not only exceed your highest hopes but to make a meaningful difference in the world.

SAY YES
TO
YOU

I'll never forget the day I walked into my boss's office to tell her I was moving to another state. I had been at Hallmark almost half my life, and I had always made my commitment to the brand's mission and the company's goals unquestionably clear. As I said the words, this incredibly composed woman turned a deep shade of pink, cradled her face in her hands, and said, "You're kidding me." I knew this would be unwelcome news. To her credit, she recovered right away and began listening intently as I explained that even though I was leaving Missouri, I didn't want to leave Hallmark.

Essentially, I was asking her if I could continue to work as vice president of product innovation from my home in another state, and travel to Kansas City every other week for important meetings and to be with my team in person. To some of you, this sounds like no big deal. Traveling may be the nature of your work. But that's not how Hallmark has operated. Hallmark is a relationship company. The brand is about emotional connections, and the company culture follows suit. While we had some individual contributors who worked offsite, as well as a few executives who lived in other states but spent the majority of their time in our offices, I would be the first senior leader who lived and worked in another state, yet led a team of direct reports in Kansas City.

I continue to be grateful to my boss for agreeing to forge new ground with me. It's been a couple of years since then. And as my responsibilities have changed, I've been able to navigate this brave new world with the support of my family, my colleagues, and, of course, technology.

In truth, I may never know exactly what my boss was thinking that day. But I'm guessing that it had something to do with the fact that I was being groomed for the next level of leadership. It was part of my vision too. What I didn't know then was how near this opportunity really was. Less than six months after I revealed my intent to move, the position I'd been working toward became available. I'll admit: This news left me breathless at first. My personal choice to move meant I would not reach my own professional mountaintop as I had once defined it. And it was *so* close. On the surface, I should have had a meltdown—regretted my decision, changed my mind, and tried to renegotiate. But I didn't—for two reasons.

First, one of them has to do with a bit of advice I often share with others: Your vision for your career should never be perpetually confined to one concrete path. If I believed that the only way I could ever achieve my professional high bar was through that one position (or the only time I had to achieve it was *now*), I probably would have sunk into a deep depression. In addition to knowing that my purpose is not specific to one position, I believe my talents and experiences are transcendent. That is, the

> 66 *Your vision for your career should never be perpetually confined to one concrete path.* 99

good I was designed to do can be used in multiple ways and in multiple places. The same is true for you. As the realization of my changing plan sunk in, knowing this for myself brought peace. And it also required that I lean heavily on God's promises. "All things work together." Romans 8:28.

The second, and most important, reason I didn't melt down was the reason I moved in the first place: I was a divorced mom of three young children, balancing single motherhood with high-level leadership, home ownership, and no blood relatives in a 1,200-mile radius. And I had met the man of my dreams. We planned to marry, which meant merging our families into a household of seven people. Because of this and many other factors, I realized the most reasonable thing to do was move to the state where he lived.

With these reasons as the basis for my decision, how could I regret it? My beliefs and values start and end with serving and inspiring others, and the most important people in my life are my husband and my children. It was critically important for me to help establish a new family for all of us. On one hand was a long hoped-for promotion, plus all the bells and whistles that go along with it. But on the other hand was the promise of love, partnership, hope, adventure, and emotional stability. There was no choice really.

Now I'm not superhuman. I had to remind myself of this truth a time or two—or seven. And there was a mourning period about that job for sure. I also had to talk my mother off a ledge—not really, but she felt badly about the missed opportunity.

But here's the thing—if I had not been clear about my beliefs and values, which define my priorities, I would still be second-guessing myself today. Instead, my purpose is being fulfilled in ways I couldn't have anticipated. My beliefs and values guided me to walk through new doors as they became visible even though I had other plans. This is why a plan without a vision, a vision without a purpose, and a purpose that is not grounded in beliefs and values is insufficient.

Knowing and clarifying all of the above for yourself allows you to have a plan while staying open to making new choices as they arise. As long as you have your priorities straight and stay true to what really matters, you can't go wrong. You might be tested, but, ultimately, you will pass. You might be delayed, but you won't be derailed. If you keep walking forward, making choices in accordance with who you are and what you value, you will find yourself exactly where you belong, doing exactly what you're meant to do. Don't be afraid to lead with purpose, on purpose. Honoring yourself is one of the most authentic ways of saying yes to you.

5

Define Your Differentiated Value: Skills, Experience, Competencies

*F*or every job you do, a core set of skills is required. These skills are the price of entry for a job well done. But I believe each person has differentiated value—unique skills, experiences, and competencies that set her apart. Your mission is to identify yours. It's important that you understand what makes you especially effective. When you do, you can intentionally line up your strengths with your future opportunities, and others can help you. But if you can't pin down what sets you apart, others won't know either. And if they don't know, they can't help you get in line.

Let me be clear about what I mean by differentiated. If you're in a financial analyst role, the fact that you have strong financial acumen or P&L management experience does not differentiate you. For this context, financial acumen is a core skill, and P&L management is a core experience. If you don't have those skills or aren't making it your business to learn them, you won't last long in that job.

If, however, you're a financial analyst for a product-development team, and you have developed product before, your understanding of the work will make you much more effective in the analyst role. Because you understand the process, the trade-offs, and the marketplace considerations through the lens of a consumer, and because you can connect these factors to financial goals, you will bring a balanced perspective to your work. You can make stronger decisions and provide more insightful guidance. In the analyst role, having developed product is differentiated experience that can set you apart. You are now a more valuable financial analyst. Moreover, you are a thought leader, and you are adding incremental value to your team.

Use Your Nature to Set Yourself Apart

So how do you recognize your differentiated value? Let's begin by considering Kara's experience.

Kara started her career in sales and received multiple awards. She's extremely goal-oriented, has excellent follow-through, and uses her God-given power of persuasion to build relationships and win over people. She's a bit of a fixer and resourceful at finding the answer to just about any question. I would consider her abilities to solve problems and to line up resources both differentiated skills that played well in sales and instilled a great deal of confidence in her clients.

There are many smart people who can't solve their way out of a paper bag unless the instructions are written on the inside. Kara is not one of those people. She also prides herself on being responsible, timely, and organized. She moves through life this way as naturally as she breathes. She can't help it. She organizes her spices. Her shoes. Her clothes. She planned her wedding. Her house. Her motherhood journey. It's all quite admirable.

After a few years, Kara entered a product-management role, where she was perceived as a bright employee and a hard worker who would do what was needed to "get the job done." This is by no means a bad thing, but it's not what people say about women on the career watch list. "A hard worker who does what it takes" is how leaders describe strong utility players—this person can conquer anything, and leaders can be confident she won't drop any balls or miss any details.

In sales, Kara's differentiated skills set her above the rest. In product management, the qualities that set an employee apart are things like strategic agility, team leadership, influence in all directions (down, across, and up), vision and imagining (seeing future opportunities where others don't), and executive presence (composure, command skills). Kara may very well have some of these skills, but in this context, her personal brand was that of a really smart, really hard worker.

Kara recently moved into a project-management role, and knowing what I know about project managing for product developers, I can make a few assumptions about how Kara will set herself apart:

- Kara will go to work every day and structure, plan, and organize projects. She will flawlessly communicate the details and requirements of these projects. She will solve challenging problems and figure out how to move resources. She will make things go, and barring any completely unrealistic productivity expectations, she will feel like she's not working. That's because this is what she does for free, every day, naturally.

- Kara will add differentiated value to this role. She will do this because she has planned product before. She understands the rhythm of it, the requirements, the must-haves versus the nice-to-haves, the people who should be involved and when, and the cost implications. She will solve problems people don't even know they have yet, because her experience will help her see issues other project managers may not see.

- People will love working with Kara. She's truly a relationship woman. She's fun and funny, committed, warm, and generous. Her team will sing her praises for a job well done, and she won't know why they're making a fuss. She will probably think, "Doesn't everybody work this way?" No, they don't. But she does. And she will be loved for it.

The story above illustrates the power of using your natural abilities to develop your differentiated value, and the importance of aligning your abilities, your passions, and your work.

Another great example of this alignment principle comes to life in the story of Subriana, a seasoned African-American executive who's made a name for herself in the multicultural marketing space. She runs her own business now, and clients from diverse industries hire her to help them grow their businesses in tandem with the changing landscape of America.

Make Your Passion Your Brand

Early in Subriana's career, she did what many women of color do. She put her head down, focused on the tasks at hand, and worked hard.

Really hard. Her brand was most likely "really hard worker," and while working hard is respectable, as we've discussed, it seldom leads to promotion. Subriana realized that the skill set she used to climb the middle-management ladder made her an effective and sought-after middle manager.

However, as she readied herself for an executive role, it became evident that her strong and varied skills were now considered table stakes. Her unique combination of demonstrated results and successful projects would get Subriana to the door of executive leadership, but they would not walk her through it. For that, she had to prove she could lead, craft a vision, as well as a strategy, and turn that vision into a reality. Finally, she had to prove that she could inspire others to do the same. She now had to market herself differently.

Subriana made a conscious decision to leverage her passion for culture to expand her personal brand. As a Black woman, it never surprised anyone when she spoke intelligently about the African-American consumer. It was when she represented the unique needs and dynamics of the Asian or Hispanic consumer that colleagues took notice.

She developed an elevator speech for this budding expertise and would intentionally connect dots between her day job and the implications of the changing shopper landscape. She figured out how to integrate multiculturalism and highlight its importance with every endeavor, and eventually, this expertise became central to her brand—not only at PepsiCo where she worked for eight years, but also in the industry.

Subriana was a founding member of the Women of Color organization at PepsiCo and later cochair for the Frito Lay chapter. These roles gave her opportunities to demonstrate thought leadership and to motivate others. It also gave her exposure to senior management and facilitated connections that would set her up for greater influence in the future.

Subriana successfully linked her purpose, her passion, and her differentiated value to the needs of the companies for which she worked. She was living and working in the winning triangle. The next senior executive opportunity that came along was planogram segmentation and merchandising for Frito Lay. Who better to lead segmentation efforts than someone who had a reputation for understanding the various multicultural populations across the country? Subriana's commitment to practicing and publicizing her differentiated value gave her an edge, and she was promoted into the role.

Eventually, Subriana's personal brand led her to start her own sales and marketing consultancy, and most of the clients and brands who knock on her door today want to maximize their value within multicultural markets or accelerate their diversity and inclusion efforts.

To this day, Subriana has not had a single job title that included the words "diversity and inclusion" or "multicultural marketing." But for her, it's not about titles, it's about passion. She believes that when your passion becomes your brand and that brand is well communicated, your career can enjoy exponential growth. We buy brands, we sell brands, and we market brands, but seldom do we see ourselves as the most important brand we have. "Say Yes to You" is more than a catchy phrase. It's a commitment to value yourself, your needs, and your skills as much as you value your company, its goals, and your colleagues.

6

Clarify Your Vision

There was a time when leaders and human-resources professionals would ask high-potential employees which specific job or job type they were interested in and then they would systematically work toward that goal together. If this job required a certain set of skills, they would orchestrate a plan to develop them. If specific relationships needed to be established because of the leadership or hierarchy in that area, they would facilitate or suggest connections. If the employee needed visibility with a certain audience, well, that could be artfully arranged as well. All things were organized to realize a high-potential employee's aspiration if that individual was fully engaged and willing to step up.

These days, we're lucky if an organization keeps the same strategy—never mind the same structure and roles—for longer than three years. We work in a volatile business climate. Technology has completely changed the game, and the more transparent business rules become, the faster competitors figure out how to redefine them. In fact, in some industries, building a three-year plan toward landing a specific job is a total waste of time.

Because jobs are increasingly difficult to chase, I coach leaders to envision their career instead. There are a series of questions to answer, and each answer serves as a brushstroke. When you step back and look at all the brushstrokes together, they create a big picture of your ideal career experience.

It's important that you *see* your future. I'm sure you've read about the power of visualization. Maybe you've even made vision boards with a church group or friend circle. These exercises help you be specific about how you see yourself moving, speaking, responding, and behaving in an environment that you imagine is best suited for you. It's not about fantasy building. It's more like a process of getting your mind to agree with your heart's desires. And once your mind agrees, you can get in gear.

Realize Your Vision

The big-picture question:

What kind of career experience do you want to be having in three to five years?

The brushstroke questions:

1. What type of work do you want to do?

This question is really about what energizes you and supports your high-level aspirations, or your purpose. People usually answer this technically, as in teaching, accounting, or marketing. But I encourage you to be more specific. For example, if you want to teach, what does a teacher do day to day that makes you want to be one? What about teaching excites you? On the other hand, what mundane teaching tasks can you see yourself doing repeatedly—without wanting to poke your eyes out? No matter what functional role you play, there must be certain activities that, when engaged in them, will interest and inspire you to be productive. Basically, this type of work will make you feel like you're making a difference.

Some possible answers to this question are:

- Building new businesses/coming up with new ideas

- Creating efficient processes that simplify work or drive profits

- Solving complex problems

- Organizing large groups of people

- Managing a P&L/driving sustainable growth

- Motivating and inspiring others

- Developing talent

- Speaking in public

It's helpful to think about times you've felt really energized at work. What were you doing? Think about this both strategically and tactically. Were you on a team responsible for developing a new business concept? Were you helping a coworker consider a dilemma? How about creating a financial plan, or writing a company announcement? Don't hesitate to capture the small things, and if there are a few, name them all. They all help you see where your natural inclinations lie and contribute to your vision.

Here's a different way to think about it: What have you always hoped you could do? Have you ever watched a colleague perform a certain function and wished you could participate, steadily thinking of ideas to improve the situation? Of course, you have to be realistic. I've marveled at gymnasts flying through the air at Cirque de Soleil, but I'm not going to add acrobatics to my list of the type of work I want to be doing. Your vision must be grounded in a core set of abilities or skills.

This takes us to the next question.

2. What skills do you want to use?

This question is not completely distinct from the question above, but it can uncover new information on a tactical level. It also can help with alignment to jobs you're exploring, as the required skills should be listed in the description.

When you feel most fulfilled at work (or at home or doing community service), what skills are you using? There are probably skills for which you receive the most praise, and with which you get the best results and feel most effective. You may not even be conscious of them, because they come so naturally for you. Some of these skills may be so innate, that when someone else labels it a skill, you think you're just being yourself. What are those skills?

For me, I feel most useful and fulfilled when I'm coaching people and sharing ideas with an audience. So, for me, that means I want to use my coaching skills via personal-insight development or identification, plus my presentation skills. This has been solidified for me not only by the way I feel when I'm performing these skills, but also by the feedback I've received from others.

However, perhaps there are skills you haven't had an opportunity to use, so the above discovery practice won't work for you. Instead, consider whether you have frustrated skills. Some people went to school for one thing, but their professional experience has not been in their field of study. This can lead to pent-up frustration and atrophy of those learned skills or concepts. I had an employee who worked hard for her master's degree, but her professional experience was in an unrelated field. It can be hard to cross the bridge from learned skills to practical experience, but ways exist to make this happen.

3. What skills or competencies do you want to learn?

First, consider your passion. When I was in creative editorial, I wanted to learn more about design. I had a general affinity for it, though I knew it would never be my leading skill. But I respected it, was inspired by it, and wanted to know enough to be a more effective product-development leader. I started learning about design from my place at that time—on the word side of things—by being present at design approvals, watching my art-director partners make decisions, and noticing how designers responded and adjusted their work. I would make suggestions for improvement and then ask about the validity of those suggestions.

I wanted to know both how to speak the language of design and how to use that language to enhance the work we were all responsible for delivering. I spent time with my design friends and openly requested that they be my teachers. It's a good idea to have people you trust enough to answer your dumb questions. This is how people learn.

I also recommend that people take full advantage of any learning phase. Over time, I learned enough to be a welcome voice in the room, and because of my editorial background, my perspective often added something meaningfully different to the conversation. Developing aesthetic judgment on the job opened the door to my first senior management position, which tasked me to manage both editorial and design leaders. Had I not invested in learning new skills, I doubt anyone would have had the confidence to give me that opportunity. It's a good idea to ask yourself what new skills you want to learn, and to start to learn them where and how you can.

Second, fill a gap. If there is a type of work you want to do, but your skills fall short of your ability to do that work well, figure out a way to bridge the gap. You can do that in a variety of ways. Sometimes people default to advanced education. You may think you need a master's degree, a certificate, or some other kind of formal training in order to travel from one point in your career to another. Sometimes you do. Other times, formal training is not required. It's wise to uncover both the overt and the subtle expectations in your workplace for the kind of work you want to do. The key is to demonstrate the skills required to do the job well. Remember: There are many ways to create opportunities to learn new skills.

Below I offer a few ways to learn new skills or further develop frustrated ones.

- **Job rotation or swap:** Is there a lateral position in your workplace that relies on the skills you want to learn? You might consider asking your direct manager or human resources about a rotation. Rotations are great on-the-job immersion opportunities—they provide a time-bound way to learn something new in a (usually) gracious environment, meaning people don't expect you to know everything right away.

  Anytime you're in a new situation—new department, company, position, team, etc.—practice what's called "beginner's mind." I've watched countless employees walk into a new situation, wanting everyone to think they know exactly what they're doing. They are afraid to ask questions for fear of seeming inadequate. They don't reach out to others to learn about processes, context, and expectations. Instead, they just quietly trudge ahead, hoping they'll figure it out. Do not do this! Ask all the questions you have when you have them. If you don't, you'll still be struggling six months later, and by then, everyone expects you to know what you're doing. That's a problem that can be avoided.

- **Job shadowing:** Job shadowing works best when you mostly need to understand how something works. You can ask a colleague who works in a given area if you can tag along for a period of time. See if she will let you attend her meetings or observe her on the job. As you shadow, write down questions and schedule time with your mentor later to get those questions answered.

Another spin on this is the good-old exploratory interview. Schedule time with a few colleagues who are doing the kind of work you want to do in order to understand what's required. Exploratory interviews will help you discern the must-haves from the nice-to-haves, and these will help you understand the most critical skill-building opportunities.

- **Special projects:** Taking on a special project is one of the best ways to learn and demonstrate new skills. There are usually multiple special initiatives going on at any time requiring cross-divisional involvement and expertise. In fact, I've never heard of a workplace where the only work available is what's on your job description. In the "Say Yes to More Work" section, I explore the benefits of special projects in more detail. But for now, just know that telling your leaders which skills you'd like to build and that you're open to special projects is a smart move. It works, and if you perform well, you'll not only learn something new, you'll *show* and *prove* at the same time.

- **Volunteer/community service:** Tremendous leadership opportunities are available in your community. Organizations always need strong and willing leaders to help organize, facilitate, plan, strategize, keep books, engage people, and so on. In fact, many types of work that people do on the job are being performed at nonprofits and other community-based programs. Volunteering is a great way to make a difference, develop your leadership skills, and make lasting connections—all at the same time.

4. What kind of workplace culture do you prefer?

Few people give this question much thought. An employee may enter a new career situation thinking about pay, advancement opportunities, brand mission, or even the ability to make a positive difference. But workplace culture is something we often think about too late—after we realize we are living or working in an environment that clashes with who we are. I'm not really talking about beliefs and values here. That's a bigger question, and we've already talked about that. What I'm referring to is the overall workplace vibe, and how that vibe fits—or doesn't fit— with your own personal groove.

Blaze a New Trail

Let's look at an example of a cultural misalignment: Ever since she was a child, Rachel showed an extraordinary aptitude for science and math. These subjects came naturally to her, and as she approached high school graduation, she was encouraged to pursue engineering. Engineering is a respectable field, and, if you play your cards right, it's a profitable one. And because it's also a white, male-dominated field, Black women who break through are regarded as trailblazers.

Rachel earned her chemical engineering degree and spent more than a decade working in technical fields. She wore her position as a badge of honor, and she truly enjoyed the work. There were times, though, when she felt out of place.

One day, Rachel attended a team-building session where a personality-type indicator was used to assess working styles and provide insights into how diverse team members can work together more effectively. During the session, participants were grouped by communication, decision-making, learning and teaching styles. Every exercise found Rachel on the opposite end of the spectrum from her team.

By the end of the day, she realized her personality and preferences vehemently disagreed with not only the other individuals with whom she worked, but also with the very culture of engineering. She honestly wasn't sure what to make of this discovery. What about her badge of honor? What about the fact that all of her work experiences had been technical?

After swimming in anxiety for a couple of weeks, she sought counsel. Her executive coach asked her to think about these questions:

- What would you do for free?

- What skills do you want to use?

- What actions do you need to take to live this passion every day?

- What skills do you want/need to learn?

Rachel also asked me for advice. We talked about her passion, what energized her, and what she wanted to experience. I advised her to clarify her vision and to share it with others. I reminded her that people can't help her if they don't know what she wants.

After some introspection, Rachel realized that almost all of her volunteer work involved public speaking, providing leadership coaching, and serving on boards. She was already doing what she loved for free. And it was the kind of work that filled her bucket enough to go to her "real job" and perform her duties as assigned.

Armed with this understanding, she decided she wanted to develop leaders. While she had some experience doing this, it wasn't focused or deliberate, and because it was something she did on the side, it wasn't a substantial amount of experience. Rachel was determined to change that, so she asked to teach a leadership course in the Learning & Development (L&D) group at her company. They needed the help and were happy to have her.

During that assignment, she learned she had an edge. Rachel was direct yet caring when she pushed people to think differently about themselves and their professional circumstances. She was also funny—the audience always had a good time listening to her, engaging with her, exploring their own ideas, and challenging themselves. Within a short period of time, Rachel began consistently achieving the highest effectiveness scores of any facilitator. Not long after performing well as a volunteer, the facilitator job became available, and the L&D director asked her to join the team. Rachel felt like she was living the dream. She was able to come to work, inspire people, and push them to think new thoughts. And she received high praise from the clients she served. She was at the top of her game, actively using her talents to make an impact on the lives of leaders and truly feeling valued.

Just when it seemed she had found her forever position, the bottom fell out. Rachel's clients were pleased with her, but her style conflicted with her division's culture, or at least with a handful of its influential leaders. She was direct and they preferred a gentler approach. She was always pushing harder for progress. They favored a more incremental evolution. She was also perceived as too funny. Rachel found herself on a performance improvement plan. All feedback from outside the division was extremely positive, but she now felt that being her authentic self was a liability.

Rachel took to heart my advice about sharing her vision. She mentioned to a client that her role within the organization was not working, but that she loved leadership development and aspired to do it full time at a higher level. The client had her own leadership development company. As God would have it, the client was currently searching for a vice president of her training organization and had been turned down by her top candidate earlier that day. Through a series of short interactions, Rachel landed the job. Today, she travels the world, delivering keynote addresses and teaching leadership courses. Her direct and humorous style sets her apart. And her passion shines through every time she stands before a group. In fact, she is the only person I know who receives standing ovations after a full day of training.

Culture can make or break your ability to succeed in doing what you love. In Rachel's case, she'd nailed her differentiated value. She was living her passion, making a difference in the lives of leaders and was aligned with her purpose, but the way she went about doing it was out of step with the cultural norm. She recognized that her abilities were not confined to one company. And by staying focused on her vision, she continued to believe her way to a more conducive environment.

So, what about you? Do you thrive on collaboration, or do you prefer an environment where everyone is clear about the distinct roles they play? Are you comfortable in a relatively flat organization where people work across the company to make decisions? Or do you like getting or giving direction from the top and having it filter down? Do you like taking risks? Do you find yourself excited and challenged when faced with a major dilemma that people look to you to sort out? Do you not only tolerate ambiguity but thrive in it? Do you bore easily, preferring a fast-paced environment? Are you happy in a casual or more formal environment?

Have you identified the best workplace cultural fit for you? Here are a few attributes to consider:

- Collaborative
- Iterative/Adaptive
- Rigorous
- Individual work
- Team based
- High risk, growth based
- Low risk, self sustaining

- Fast paced
- Methodical
- Ambiguous
- Process driven
- Creative
- Casual
- Formal

Leverage Your Broad-Spectrum View

I met Sally Helgesen during a National Association of Female Executives (NAFE) conference in Minneapolis in 2014. She was delivering a keynote based on her new book, *The Female Vision: Women's Real Power at Work*, and I was teaching a workshop called "Making Vision Real," inspired by her topic.

Listening to Sally's talk that day transformed me. She taught us about perceptions associated with women and vision, differences between how men and women absorb information, and how women can and should leverage our unique visioning skills to strengthen our companies and ourselves. She gave me words for gut feelings I'd had countless times but could never quite explain.

Sally became interested in the subject of vision as a tool for business success and career development in 2008. That's when she came across two global research studies by INSEAD and the

Washington Quality Group on senior executives' perceptions of women's leadership skills. While both studies found that senior leaders in large international companies valued female employees' skills in relationship-building, motivating teams, communicating, and negotiating, they tended to rank the women low when it came to vision. They defined vision as big-picture, long-term future focus in the service of organizational success. One study also found that women, in an interesting twist, rated themselves quite high on vision, in contrast to their more typical low assessment of their own skills. Curious about the reason for both the perception and the discrepancy, Sally—along with coauthor Julie Johnson—set off to find out more.

Drawing on interviews, case studies, and documented historical examples, Sally and Julie became convinced that women's capacity for noticing things operates somewhat differently than men's capacity—and that this difference lies at the root of men's and women's varied visions. This thesis was supported by solid lab research documenting gender differences in how people notice conducted by neuroscientists at Yale, Columbia, and UCLA.

Using Functional MRIs that map the brain, researchers found that male brains typically notice or respond to one thing at a time, in a sequential pattern. In other words, men notice things like a laser. Female brains scan the environment for a broad range of clues, processing many points of information at the same time. Women notice things more like a radar.

This difference in perception can make it difficult for men to understand a woman's attempt to communicate her vision. To a focused "noticer," stories women tell about what they perceive to be important may sound disjointed or off topic. Since men's skills and ways of being in and seeing the world have shaped organizations for so long, many businesses place a high value on focused notice and consider it a leadership behavior. When a woman operates from her broad-spectrum notice, she can be perceived as lacking vision altogether, which can be an impediment when being evaluated as a potential leader.

As Sally conducted her research, she began to wonder if there were ways to help women articulate their ideas more persuasively, and to brand themselves as having stronger, more comprehensive visions. She also felt she could help organizations more appropriately evaluate women's visions, and wrote *The Female Vision* as a way to support both women and companies as they work to drive results.

Sally cites the 2008 financial crisis as a perfect example of how dismissing women's vision can be not only shortsighted but sometimes devastating. Citing author Michael Lewis's now-famous observation that "the remarkable thing about the financial crisis was how little women had to do with it," she notes that a number of high-profile female financial executives foresaw the impending crisis and warned their institutions or the public about it. They were either dismissed as gloom-and-doom Cassandras or lost their jobs. These women had noticed contextual factors and, thus, anticipated an unraveling that their male colleagues, focused purely on the numbers, ignored.

Sally believes that organizations can benefit greatly from understanding the role broad-spectrum notice can play, not only in managing talent but in evaluating risk, allocating resources, and making strategic decisions. "A broad and contextual perspective, balanced with a focused and analytical understanding, is what a fast-changing global economic environment requires," she says.

Thanks to environmental change, technological advances, and the global economy, we are increasingly affected by what's going on in other parts of the world. Focused vision is insufficient in such a complex society. Sally asserts that women are in a strong position to bring forward perspectives often lacking in the business world.

But before we do, we have to recognize our capacity for radar vision and be able to articulate its value. Below are Sally's three practical tips for making your vision work for you, and for your business.

1. **Recognize the value in your vision and stand behind it.** It's very common for a woman to share an observation in a strategic discussion and immediately feel like she is off base when focused "noticers," i.e., men, don't agree. She may think, "Maybe I wasn't supposed to notice that." She internalizes their response, rather than understanding why what she notices is important (and what the implications are) and having the courage to defend it.

2. **Take time to assess your vision.** If you decide to take your observations seriously and present your vision up the chain of command, make sure you think it through carefully in advance. We've all had smart ideas that come from noticing lots of things and synthesizing them, but sometimes women share the outcome prematurely. We need to think through possible objections and prepare for them, instead of assuming that other people will get it and simply backing off when they don't. One of the most self-defeating responses women have to being

dismissed is this: "They just don't get it." We should instead think, "How do I help them get it, given what I know about them?"

3. **Consider how to communicate your vision.** Sally says it can make focused people uncomfortable to not have a vision explained, but we can help others connect the dots. Those who think exclusively about numbers need to be shown why something else is important. We have to learn to calibrate our language—not just accommodate our audience—and to bring them along to a larger vision. Sometimes we need to start with data in order to help people see why they should care.

Sally always cautions that many exceptions exist to the rule. There are men who have broad-spectrum notice and women who are focused noticers. "Many women have figured this out intuitively, but twenty-five years in the leadership-development space have taught me that women tend to learn these principles relatively late in their careers. It's helpful to recognize them earlier, and use them to help both emerging women and men make the most of the female vision," Sally notes.

Sally's professional purpose is to give people hope and to help them know they're part of something important. In business, "seeing around the corners" is more valuable than ever. Women can add significant strategic value to the business world—we just have to be clear about what value we're adding and thoughtful about how we add it.

Your Turn

Now that you've had an opportunity to think about what you really want to do and what skills you have—or will need—in order to do it, you're ready to take a crack at drafting your career vision. I hope you can start to see your own big picture coming together before your eyes. A professional discovery like the one outlined here can propel you toward your goals by clarifying the many assumptions you may have been carrying with you about your best path forward. Now—write your vision statement:

In three years, I aspire to be (doing type of work) in a (cultural description) environment, leveraging my (skills used/differentiated value) and learning (new skills) so that I can achieve (your purpose).

Your vision is valuable at work and to your own professional development. Can you see your own future with a broad-spectrum view?

7

Create Your Plan

Disclaimer alert: Don't take the below principles as literal instruction. In fact, if anyone tries to sell you "Five Sure-Fire Steps to Getting the Career You Want," run away fast.

There is no foolproof way to get the career you want. But there are principles you can use to do so. There are proven approaches to help you deconstruct your vision into actionable parts. A vision is actionable—we just don't always see it that way. I've always said that a vision without a plan is a fantasy. Of course, fantasies are a dime a dozen! To be honest, I have no interest in inspiring you to dream big for your work life, then leaving you floating in the clouds with no path to achieving that dream. If you can't take the principles shared in this book and go do something tangible with them, I haven't given you anything of value.

Although living your professional purpose will take thought and hard work on your part, it's not rocket science. It doesn't have to be confusing or overly theoretical. It can be *real*. If you try to think of just three actions you can take to realize each component of your vision, you can turn your dream into a practical reality. The cumulative effect of making a few moves across a few fronts is surprisingly effective. You don't have to conquer the world in one fell swoop. You just have to take focused action toward your destiny and watch how things come together.

Below is a sample vision. I've underlined each component, so you can clearly see how to deconstruct a vision and how to plan each part.

(1) <u>In three years</u>, I aspire to be (2) <u>coaching and speaking across the country about professional development</u> in a (3) <u>flexible and forward-thinking</u> environment, leveraging my (4) <u>human insight, relationship-building skills, and ability to motivate and inspire</u> and learning to (5) <u>operationalize my passion</u> so that I can achieve (6) <u>my dream of helping women realize their own professional purpose.</u>

1. The Time Horizon: "In three years…"

Set your time horizon. If you're in a corporate environment, this is important for a few reasons. First of all, it helps you avoid the impatience trap, which can sometimes appear to top leadership as blind ambition. If you know your goal is to have a certain experience three years from now, you won't ask your boss every week in staff meetings when your promotion is coming. Bosses hate that. When we do this, it seems we want to be promoted for the title or money, or both. (This may be true for you, but it serves no one for your boss to believe it!) Your leaders want to know what you're passionate about, how you desire to contribute, why, and what you're willing to give for the good of the organization. To whom much is given, much is required. So when leaders think you are more concerned with getting than giving, it's no *bueno*.

I don't believe for a second that aspiring leaders are more concerned with getting than giving. I believe that sometimes we haven't done the long-range visioning and planning that helps us chart our course toward our goals over a reasonable period of time. A reasonable period is one that allows for timing and opportunity to come together in a way that aligns with your aspirations. If you stay silent about your ambitions, get tired of waiting, and start to push, leaders can feel blindsided. They need time to help you get ready, to plant seeds of promise with their peers, and to coordinate efforts in support of your goals. Sometimes this can happen swiftly, but sometimes it can take a year or longer. The more you know about your goals and your development needs, and the sooner you know it, the more your manager can help you.

Reasonable time horizons offer you a chance to gather blocks of experience, build relationships, and/or develop skills that will be critical to enabling your vision. In my case, a time horizon gave me a chance to write this book.

Which three seeds will you plant in the next six weeks?

1. _____

2. _____

3. _____

2. Type of work: "coaching and speaking across the country about professional development…"

We clarified the type of work you want to do earlier in this chapter. But here's where you decide how you will prepare yourself to do it. Find out where this work is currently being done and schedule exploratory interviews with people who are doing it. What you really need is a deep understanding of what success looks like. Who's considered top talent in this area? Why? What skills or behaviors do they have that make them successful? What can you learn about best practices? Look externally for inspiration here, and develop a well-rounded point of view. What you're trying to do now is learn what it will take to position yourself to do this work.

You may discover you have everything you need and all that remains is informing others and making connections. But it's possible, even probable, that you will discover gaps—skills, behaviors, experiences, or even perceptions—that need to be filled. In my case, I sought counsel from people in the publishing industry. I've been writing since I was a child and even have a few books published, but not in the business success category. Know the difference between doing the work and doing it well.

What three actions will you take to find out what is required to achieve your vision?

1. _____

2. _____

3. _____

3. Cultural environment: "flexible and forward-thinking…"

As mentioned earlier in this chapter, this topic mostly requires intentional thought. You may never find the perfect culture, but you should understand key attributes of a culture you could thrive in and identify your must-haves. For example, if you're the primary caretaker for your family, one of your must-haves may be flexibility. If you're a "maximizer" type—a person whose best work comes when you're making other people's ideas stronger—you might thrive in a collaborative culture where no hard lines exist between functional responsibilities.

Whatever your must-haves are, initiating these conversations before a misalignment occurs is always the best approach. Equally important are the cultural attributes that make you absolutely crazy. I strongly encourage you not to dive headlong into a culture that is completely counter to you. You may believe you can overcome a poor culture fit in favor of other benefits, but as Peter Drucker once said and a colleague of mine frequently reminds us, "Culture eats strategy for breakfast." Don't end up hungry because you never gave this topic enough thought.

What three actions will you take to find out what culture fits you best?

1. _____

2. _____

3. _____

4. Differentiated value: "human insight, relationship-building skills, and ability to motivate and inspire…"

You've already gone through the process of identifying your differentiated value. Now is the time to name ways to provide visibility for the skills that set you apart. If you're an extraordinary innovator, which brainstorm sessions will you arrange invitations to so you can expand your reputation in this space? What ideas will you bring forward that no one requested, but for which you will become valuable? Often our differentiated value is at our very core. In other words, it doesn't only show up in a specific job but transcends positions and adds value across many needs and opportunities. You now know your differentiated value. Who else needs to know it? And how are you going to show them?

What three actions will you take to provide visibility for your unique abilities?

1. _____

2. _____

3. _____

5. Skills needed: "to operationalize my passion…"

This might be the most time- and energy-intensive part of actualizing your vision. That's because it involves learning things that are not necessarily intuitive for you, so they require conscious effort and additional resources. If it were intuitive, you would probably be doing it already, and it wouldn't be a gap.

You can deal with skill gaps in a number of ways. We talked at length about the various ways to bridge the gap between your current abilities and those required in your own personal promised land. Now you have to decide which of these tactics you will pursue. Will you lobby for a project that allows on-the-job training? Will you go back to school? Will you find a mentor with a reputation for excellence in your area of development? If you're already a manager, will you learn the skill basics but surround yourself with experts so that, ultimately, the need is still met? The options are endless and can be overwhelming, depending on the distance between here and there. But it's only overwhelming until you take the first step. Just start moving in the right direction, and you will reach your destination.

Which three actions will you take to fill your skill gap?

1. _____

2. _____

3. _____

6. Purpose: "my dream of helping women realize their own professional purpose…"

The most important thing you can do here is remain aware. Don't lose sight of your purpose. Your purpose grounds you and keeps you focused. Sometimes, it's the key to your sanity. When you're not advancing as quickly as you had hoped, purpose-driven work makes the wait time well spent. When recognition is slow to show up, purpose-driven work rewards you anyway. When you're tired of pushing, purpose-driven work is a resting place. Everything looks different when you're working toward your purpose. Ask yourself: What can I do to live out my purpose more effectively? Knowing your purpose and living it, every day, empowers you like nothing else.

Work Your Plan

Now that we've deconstructed your vision and you have a plan, how will you keep yourself accountable to working that plan? You are a wise investment. Treat your own career like the most important business goal you've ever been asked to deliver. You're worth it.

Ready for another inspirational story? Yesi Morrillo-Gual has mastered the arts of planning and execution. Her approach may seem rigorous for some, but she gets it done. She is a wife, mother of two, executive director, and founder and CEO of a women's leadership network called Proud to Be Latina. She's also in the midst of acquiring her fourth degree. Oh, and she's writing a novel. I know, take a breath already. I had to ask her how on earth she does all of this—I thought my life was complicated!

Yesi has a weekly and daily schedule in her planner. She doesn't necessarily believe in resolutions. Instead, she places value on making forward progress every day. Her current goal is to focus more on her personal well-being, so she recently updated her weekly schedule to incorporate more self-care.

According to Yesi, goals should be practical. Can you physically and emotionally do what you want *and* fulfill your other responsibilities? This question isn't about letting yourself off the hook or settling. It's more like, "Can Tara, at forty years old, be a supermodel in Italy and a working, traveling author/wife/mother of six children?" The answer is no, by the way. Also, I'm 5'4", but that's another issue.

Yesi breaks her goals into segments and assigns target deadlines to them. She writes down the tasks for each segment and literally works from her list. She commits to putting her goals on paper and sticking to deadlines. Sometimes, she says, if we don't see something, it's not real. Then we make all the excuses in the world as to why we never get something done.

Have you ever heard about someone launching an idea you've been sitting on and thought, "that could've been me!" (We all have.) Yesi's philosophy is this: If you set targets and stick to them, that will be you. But she adds that being realistic is key. There's no greater threat to a project than an impossible deadline. It's defeating for all involved.

She also recommends an accountability partner. Identify someone who will ask you how your goals are progressing. As far as her novel is concerned, she strives to write forty-five minutes or one thousand words every day. If she projects this pattern into the future, she will have a first draft in one hundred days.

Reduce Life's Little Distractions

Yesi's final gem of insight on planning and productivity was probably the one I found most profound. She told me about an experiment she conducted to understand the true impact of life's little distractions.

Social media, smartphones, and news—the moments we spend checking these items can seriously detract from our progress. For one full day, Yesi wrote down every time she checked email, social media, or her phone. In ten hours, she checked one of these forms of media thirty times, which equaled three-and-a-half hours of her ten-hour day. That's more than thirty percent! What's more, she admitted that not one of those emails or texts was important or urgent. Essentially, she wasted her time. That blew my mind (and convicted me too)!

How can you detach long enough to ensure you get things done? What does a new level of discipline, planning, and productivity look like for you? Planning is important, but working your plan is equally important.

8

Balance Work and Life

*T*here are countless women in America who declare motherhood as their life calling. For them, there is no separate professional aspiration outside of this core purpose—at least while they're raising their children. There may be times they long for a change of pace—having an adult conversation, sleeping in past 6 a.m., taking a trip with friends—but generally, they're secure in their roles and feel their experience is in line with who they want to be. They don't work outside the home. And that's perfectly okay.

There are also women who are completely committed to their careers, their husbands, or their personal passions. They don't have children, but this doesn't mean there aren't beloved children in their lives. For those who choose not to be parents, the spontaneity that allows—the ability to chase dreams or be still when they feel like it—is preferable. And that's perfectly okay too.

There are other women who move between these roles every day. These moms work outside the home, and they likely have—at one time or another—doubted whether the path they're walking can really work long term.

If you fall into this third category, as I do, you've likely driven to work wrought with guilt over a little person you've left with a caregiver. You've cringed over missing a once-in-a-lifetime first or a baseball game while you traveled for work. You've judged yourself harshly for the pizza you picked up after your 6 p.m. meeting, because you didn't have time or energy to cook for your family—again. You've told yourself—maybe in a whisper during a moment of weakness, or maybe in a holler on repeat—that there is no way to survive, to care for your family, to provide them the best life possible if you don't make painful sacrifices. But sometimes you resent the feeling that comes with making the only choice you believe you have. You move through life feeling like you're doing lots of things but nothing especially well. At some point during the cycle of madness, you feel like a pawn in a game you just can't win.

Well, here's a news flash: You can have professional satisfaction *and* be a great mother.

I'm not stating this as a casual observer. When I was twenty-five, I gave birth to my first child—a beautiful, quiet-natured girl who hardly made a sound. She was alert, observant, and smelled delicious, like all babies do. My then-husband and I agreed that I would take six months' maternity leave. For the first four months, I couldn't imagine ever leaving her. I didn't want to stop holding her, rocking her to sleep, and looking into her bright eyes for hours on end. This was my life, and I was perfectly happy living it.

Just after the four-month mark, in a shift that surprised even me, I got restless. I grew curious about what my colleagues were up to. By the time my six-month leave was up, I was quite ready to go back to work. I realized during my time away that my professional life was really important to me. It was energizing, intellectually fulfilling, and kept me in a constant state of learning, which is where I prefer to be.

Just as I started getting the hang of the working-mom thing, I got pregnant again. This time, I gave birth to my first son, who was a lot more demanding than my daughter. He was a bundle of emotion, otherwise known as a mix of heart-warming benefits and mind-numbing challenges. During his younger years, his sensitivity was all consuming. I'm proud to say, as he ages, I see his sensitivity translate into compassion and emotional intelligence that rivals that of some adults.

I went back to work four months after my son was born, and weeks later, I was promoted into my first people-management job. I had twenty-two direct reports, many of whom had been at Hallmark up to four times as long as I had. I was twenty-seven years old and leading the editorial staff for our largest business. My manager at the time, who was hailed as the queen of editorial, became my first work-life role model. Some wondered how she was able to go home at 5 p.m. every day when they were working late. She was a seasoned professional and had earned her reputation for excellence many times over, so others' opinions of her schedule were of no concern to her. She was effective and respected. No balls were ever dropped on her watch. Those of us who paid attention learned everything from her, not the least of which was how to have a life while you worked. It's critical that women leaders in the workplace make choices that support their lives and their families. It sets a good example and gives other women the courage to do the same.

Three years later, I gave birth to another son. Due to multiple infections, he suffered through four months of illness. I suffered too. On several occasions, I had to excuse myself to take him to the specialist, to pick him up from daycare, or to stay home with him to ease my mind about his condition. Watching children struggle brings all else into perspective. Some mornings I asked myself, "Will I choose work or my kids?" When something is wrong with your children, the answer is obvious. But that's not always the case. Sometimes the former wins out: Make major credibility-building presentation or attend Halloween parade at school? (I'd ask myself, "Are they really going to miss me walking alongside them at the school parade when there's candy to collect, and we'll be doing it again in two days?")

A few months after my youngest was born, I was promoted to an executive leadership position. Career-wise, I was flying high—still learning, doing what I loved, and working with incredible people. As a working mom, I had found my rhythm. But when my son was just two years old, things got interesting. Long story short, I realized my marriage was over. Facing single motherhood with three young children—ages seven, five, and two—was not in my plan. At first, my ex-husband and I coparented. Then, not long after our divorce was final, he moved away for one year.

My family was on the East Coast, and I was living in the middle of the country. No grandmas, aunts, or cousins lived nearby. I had really good friends, but they worked too. I was alone, or so I thought. My year of true single parenthood was everything I feared it would be and, at the same time, everything I needed. During this trying time, I learned many valuable lessons, not the least of which is that there is no peace in trying to be Superwoman. But while superpowers may be off the table, I did discover significant personal power within me, and I soon figured out that the only way I would survive my newfound reality was to exercise that power regularly.

Design Your Life

Trudy Bourgeois, CEO of The Center for Workforce Excellence, often speaks about the importance of empowering ourselves to design the lives we want to live. She, like many others, believes that work-life balance is a myth and that the day women started writing about it, talking about it, and striving for it was the day a whole lot of trouble began.

Trudy has had her share of aha moments on her journey as a career mom. Her experience has taught her to embrace responsibility for her personal and professional choices. As an executive coach, she advises other career moms to do the same. While external influences are real and unconscious bias related to career moms' advancement persists, she says the blaming mindset is disempowering, and lessens our belief that we are in control of the ultimate relationship between our careers and our families.

I love hearing Trudy discuss this topic, because she's such a realist. In her experience, the truth about corporate America's current state pertaining to career moms can be summed up this way: It's not as good as we wish it were, and not as bad as we fear it is. It's somewhere in between.

Early in her professional career, Trudy served as a sales representative for a tobacco company. She and her husband had one son and were trying to conceive another child, but they were unable to do so for four years.

At the start of her new assignment, she discovered she was pregnant. Trudy was terrified about what her employer might think or do, so she intended to keep her pregnancy quiet for as long as possible. That was until she and her new boss ran into her doctor's wife on a business trip. Trudy was so afraid she would be outed, that she disclosed her pregnancy to her new boss. That was quickly followed by a litany of reasons why she would be the best salesperson ever and a vow that her pregnancy and family needs wouldn't interfere with her work.

Shortly thereafter, Trudy's son required surgery. Trudy was so concerned with keeping her promise to her boss that she opted not to be at the surgery in favor of a work commitment. To this day, she believes she made the wrong choice, expressing her regret simply and profoundly. "As his mother, I was not there," she says.

We each have to determine what we will protect and preserve. The good news is that life is a series of steps, and our few missteps can serve as building blocks for our future climb. Trudy's bottom line these days is clear. If your company doesn't value you, you need to rethink your commitment. You have to value yourself first. Over time, we learn to focus on the big things. We worry less about what people think and more about what we can do to affect change. Through a lens of optimism, we see that people are more understanding and compassionate than we imagine. And we learn for ourselves that we can have our work and a life, because there is no perfect "balance" that keeps still for any length of time.

I asked Trudy—a highly sought-after executive coach, speaker, trainer, and consultant—how career moms can embody their personal power more effectively. In true Trudy fashion, she offered three straightforward pieces of advice:

- **Get your mind right.** You are not a victim. You are in control. There is no *them* more powerful than *you.*

- **Don't think of choices as "yes" or "no."** Give yourself permission to reconfigure, and remember that you are on a journey. There will be crunch times, all-nighters, and unproductive days. This doesn't mean you're failing. It means you're living, in process.

- **Be present.** When you're home, be home. When you're at work, be at work. The lines will blur sometimes, but make it a habit to be present where you are.

As Trudy reminds women all the time, we shouldn't have to choose between being a good parent and being a good professional. While the business world catches up, she advises women of all generations to remember their worth, craft a vision for their lives, and have the courage to vote with their feet. If the company doesn't work for you, don't work for it.

People ask me all the time how I juggle the professional and the personal as a mother of five children at home, a wife to a husband who travels periodically, an executive traveling every other week to Kansas City, a speaker traveling to engagements, and an author. I'll be honest—I don't always do it well.

I try to cook at least five days a week, but sometimes I fall short of that goal. There are days at the end of a long week, when my children want to tell me about their latest adventures, and I want to hide under my bed and close the door. I hit a wall now and then where my energy and mindfulness are concerned. I'm a human being and I have limitations. We all do. And to be fair, my family has a few built-in support structures that make our seemingly complicated life livable. As a blended family, we coparent with two sets of extremely present, loving, and committed parents. This arrangement enables our family to thrive. We also have help with house cleaning, which means the time we spend with our kids is high quality. Lastly, my husband is my own personal Captain America, but that's a different book.

The point in sharing my personal story isn't to suggest that any career woman should or even can manage her family the way I do. It's simply a reminder that we all need some support if we want to maintain our sanity and grow our careers.

Your Turn

1. Find help.

If you don't have someone to help share the logistics of managing a household, get someone—hired help, a spouse, a friend, a family member, a neighbor, someone.

- What can you offload? And to whom?

- If it's going to cost you, what can you cut out of your budget to enable it?

2. Prioritize self-care.

A little time for you goes a long way. I'm not going to belabor this one. Countless books and articles have been written about it. Just do it. Without it, you will have less energy, less patience, and compromised mental, emotional, and physical health. Stop questioning whether you can figure it out, and just figure it out.

- When can you make time for physical activity?

- Are you able to retreat to a room in your house for one uninterrupted hour of peace every week?

- What will you do differently to preserve your own well-being?

3. Establish emotional support.

For some of us, a good vent session can recalibrate our minds. A good friend or family member who will listen and remind you of your incredible awesomeness is a must-have. We all need a boost now and then! Who can you call on when the going gets tough?

- Name the people in your support system.

- Now ask one of them overtly if she is willing to provide emotional support when needed.

4. Don't be too proud to ask for assistance.

We really struggle with this one, don't we? Society suggests that we should be able to handle all of our responsibilities on our own. This is a fallacy of the worst kind. Many career moms unconsciously accept an imposed punishment for their choice to pursue high levels of leadership. We believe parenting is our most important job, so if we choose to work on top of that (or must), we feel we somehow deserve the stress and difficulty associated with balancing the two.

Can you imagine if men had the same mindset? Can you fathom if men believed parenting were their most important job, and they had to manage their careers on top of it by *themselves*? When men were ascending to power in corporations all over the world, they had support managing their families. (That support was women, by the way.) If we want to grow into our full leadership potential, we can't do it alone. Have you ever had people offer help and refuse to take them up on it? I've done this, but I don't anymore. People wouldn't offer if they didn't want to be there for you, so put your pride on the shelf and say yes.

- For which tasks will you accept help?

- If your children are old enough, how are they helping?

- If your children are not yet helping, when can they start?

- How can you ask your children to participate in ways that will lighten your load?

5. Let some stuff go.

I live in a neighborhood where many moms stay at home. I think that's awesome, but that's not my life. I have to release the idea of being PTA president. Once in a while, I may bake cupcakes, but most often I pick up treats from the grocery store. I try to choose one field trip per school year to chaperone with the younger children and attend school parties if I can. I go to their games and concerts if I'm not traveling. I will likely never be the mom that every child in the class knows and calls by name. Would I like to be? Sometimes. But it's just not realistic. I have to let that go and find peace with it.

Since my children are a little older, I intentionally leverage opportunities to help them understand the choices I'm making. At the end of the day, children learn to live life on purpose by watching their parents. My kids have been disappointed by me a time or two. It doesn't feel good. But they've also been inspired by me and proud of me. I'm sure the same is true for you. As your children grow, the big picture will come into focus. And they won't see you as the mom who missed the science fair. They'll see you as the mom who had love to give, time to share, dreams to chase, and a life to lead. They'll see the mom who taught them, by example, that the world is their oyster.

Life is too short to live with guilt of epic proportions over whether you can be the woman you strive to be 100 percent of the time. In corporate America at least, plenty of leaders recognize how offering women true flexibility means maximum value for them. The mom who knows she can go to a recital once in a while will work at ten o'clock at night to finish a contract. The one who feels she has to choose will, over time, give less than her best. And that's expensive. If you stay, but feel conflicted, it costs your company in productivity and quality of effort. If you leave, it costs them a considerable amount of money to replace you.

Today's workplace demands creativity in how we allow people to contribute. The leaders who understand the relationship between flexibility and commitment will get the most from their women leaders over time. The ones who don't will suffer. Your job is to be consistently excellent. Theirs is to keep an open mind. Being excellent gives you the best path to expressing your work-life needs.

If you're like most career moms, there's something you hold onto—pressure, fear, guilt, stress, etc.—that serves no one, especially you. What will you let go? It can be a responsibility or even an idea.

You have to believe in your talents, your dreams, and your inherent value—both as a woman and a leader. You have to believe in your right to have balance, joy, and peace. You have to believe in your ability to win. You are absolutely worthy and capable of having an amazing career and a beautiful life. There's no reason you can't achieve your career goals if you're open, optimistic, and committed to doing so.

SECTION 3

SAY YES
TO
RISK

When you hear the word "risk," what comes to mind? In the business world, we tend to understand risk as financial, competitive, reputation-based, or otherwise connected to stability. In this sense, it's easy to buy into the notion that risk-taking is inevitable, or at least par for the course.

We're all familiar with the common workplace phrase, "The greater the risk, the greater the reward." Well, when you truly commit to advancing your professional purpose, the same can be said of personal risk. Leading with purpose and breaking through to the next level will test your personal fortitude in ways you may not anticipate, but must learn to embrace.

Personal risk is a prerequisite to the kind of growth and success many of us long to achieve. Without a doubt, this journey will require you to do some letting go, and some holding on. You'll plant many seeds, and dig up others. You'll acquire new skills, attitudes, and relationships—and surrender ideas and relationships you once thought crucial to your happiness.

> " *Personal risk is a prerequisite to the kind of growth and success many of us long to achieve.* "

In the following pages, you'll read stories of both professional and personal risk that illustrate the power of leaping into the unknown, the strength of trusting yourself to land on your feet, and the inspiration others pick up from you along the way.

9

Connect with Networks, Mentors, and Sponsors

*H*ome isn't the only place we need help. To advance your professional purpose, you will need it at work too. No one gets to the top alone. As we've discussed, somehow we've come to believe that asking for help or receiving it when offered is weak. Getting help is nothing to be ashamed of. Refusing it, on the other hand? Now that's not smart. You can't possibly know everything there is to know about how to be successful. We all need others to fill in gaps for us, to force us to think new thoughts and make new moves. Help comes in watershed moments but also in a word or note of encouragement that brings clarity. We need several kinds of help. And that's more than okay—it's wisdom in action.

Seek Common Ground

As a marketing communications representative at DuPont, Sheila Robinson was labeled a master networker. When faced with a business problem, she connected with whomever necessary to find the solution. Forging relationships came naturally to her, and her colleagues were always pleasantly surprised by not only the people Sheila engaged, but how effortlessly she enlisted them.

Women, and especially women of color, often struggle with the idea of networking. Somewhere along the way, we've reduced the notion of networking to using people. This feels inauthentic, and those of us who take pride in being genuine often develop an aversion to networking, preventing us from developing relationships that could fuel our individual and collective success.

Some of us attend networking events and judge our effectiveness by how many business cards we exchange. "We try to meet everyone in the room and walk out with one hundred business cards, feeling like we got it done," Sheila says. "That's not how you network—that's how you annoy people!"

I love Sheila's philosophy. For her, networking is about giving. It's about offering ourselves up and creating win-win opportunities. Our goal should not be to take something from another person. Instead, it should be to build a relationship that might be in our network for life. "It's about being present, with your whole self," she says.

Sheila has practical advice for women who want to become more-effective networkers. "First, clarify your personal brand," she says. "Do you know what value you bring to others?" When a company launches a new brand, they do it because they know it's worth something. Thus, says Sheila, the best approach to networking is to show up with your value in tow. When you do, there's a strong possibility you'll walk out with resources and the potential for true collaboration.

Sheila also recommends we take time to learn about the people who will be present at networking events. What are their roles, affiliations, passions, and strengths? "Look for those with whom you have something in common—people who can not only help you accomplish your goals," Sheila suggests, "but who have something to gain from your talents as well."

> **" *We need several kinds of help. And that's more than okay —it's wisdom in action.* "**

She often reminds women that we can invest years in a relationship before anything tangible develops. Genuine relationships are nurtured over time. Sheila sends written cards expressing what she specifically appreciates about the people in her network. Basically, she keeps them in mind and stays in touch. In her years as a master networker, she has discovered that if you show people love, they will return it.

I asked Sheila about the fear many people associate with networking. She feels one of the best ways to get over it is to become comfortable with the word no. To a degree, Sheila credits courage, including the willingness to deal with rejection, with her ten years of business success as founder and CEO of *Diversity Woman*, a quarterly magazine and annual conference that provides ideas, solutions, and resources through print, online, and special events to support the leadership and executive development of women of all races, cultures, and backgrounds. "N and O. These two letters paralyze people," she says. "They keep us from doing the right thing, and sometimes keep us from doing anything at all. Some people aren't going to network with you. Maybe it's not God's timing or just not meant for you. There are many reasons why a connection may not take root. If you can't create value for the person, that's not the right person."

The most valuable relationships in my current network are with people whose work I have initially respected from afar. I admired them before I ever reached out, so when I did, I was clear about how we could develop a mutually beneficial connection. These women inspire me to be better, to work harder. They freely offer their support and encouragement. They celebrate my achievements, and I celebrate theirs. Sometimes, the mutual admiration alone is an invaluable exchange of energy. But often, to Sheila's point, the value extends further. I now consider many of the women who've inspired me my friends.

Sheila notes that our lives are so full and fast-paced, that some women don't really have a lot of time for new connections. She recalls the day she met Cathie Black, former Chair and President of Hearst Corporation, at a Boston women's conference. She had identified Cathie as a person she desired to meet, but the conference took place in a huge venue and getting to her was harder than she thought.

Sheila started by attending Cathie's workshop. She tried to ask a question so Cathie would remember her, but she couldn't make her way to the microphone. She figured she might catch her afterwards, but the room was packed and Sheila couldn't get close enough. She asked the Boston conference public relations manager if she could interview her, but Cathie's schedule was too tight. Sheila remembers Cathie having a seemingly impenetrable entourage. Sheila followed her into the media room, and when Cathie walked over to grab a cup of coffee, she did too. She initiated a conversation that day in Boston, and they've been emailing each other for over a year. Cathie introduced Sheila to another woman who has been a major support to Sheila and her work, and the relationships continue to flourish.

Sometimes a great connection provides more benefits than we could ever imagine. Even if we don't have a specific request, we can always seek guidance, insights, or encouragement. If we stay focused on serving our purpose and providing value in everything we do, Sheila believes nature will take its course. To summarize Sheila's practical guide to networking—know your value, do your homework, be persistent (not annoying), and don't be afraid of the word *no*.

Mentor 1: The Peer Mentor

A peer mentor is incredibly valuable to any emerging leader. There are usually people in the office who are better connected than others, and they're not always high-level leaders. Sometimes it's an administrative assistant, a fellow middle manager, or someone who's been at the company for a long time and not only knows a lot of people, but also deeply understands the inner workings of the organization.

This person doesn't judge your questions or second-guess your intent. She or he helps teach you the rules of the road and identify roadblocks. Especially when you enter a new work environment, the peer mentor is the first one you should seek. Great companies may help make this connection as part of an on-boarding process. Each time you advance, a new peer mentor at your current level is a good thing to have.

I rely on a couple of trusted peers to regularly check my thinking. I tap into their knowledge often. And I ask outright for their advocacy when I'm trying to push something that feels new or different. They trust me, and I trust them. We have each other's backs. Whenever a woman leader tells me there is no one at her company she can go to with her questions, doubts, or flubs, and feel safe, I ask why. Sometimes it's because she's not extended herself in this way. That's fixable. But sometimes, it's because of the corporate culture.

Mentor 2: The Mirror

Your mirror mentor is someone who will encourage your humanity and tell you the truth about yourself—others' perceptions, your strengths and weaknesses, and the gifts they see in you that you may not fully appreciate. I like to think of this person as the keep-it-real-with-love mentor. She will help you face your fears and, just by being honest with you, give you the courage to optimize your high notes and develop the rest.

Women often take a great deal of pride in who we are. "I am who I am," we might say. "This is how God made me." Or perhaps, "They don't have to like me, but they have to respect me." I've heard many iterations of this statement over the years, and unfortunately, it usually comes off as a defensive reply to undesirable feedback. It's safe to say that many of the things we hang onto and define as "who we are" are superficial and sometimes unhealthy.

If you want to thrive in corporate America, you will have to learn to correlate who you are with your inherent value, not what's on the surface or how you choose to express yourself on any given day. Your introversion? That may be who you are. Your circuitous or highly linear thought process? Sure. Your tendency to verbally process information? Check. But being late to meetings? No. Biting sarcasm? Not so much.

Forgive me if I've struck a nerve, but one reason I see careers stall is an unwillingness to step back and consider the big picture. If you desire to preserve some of your claim-to-fame attributes at all costs, my question then is this: "How's that working for you?" If we repeatedly receive negative feedback on some aspect of our leadership or interpersonal approach, we should pause to reflect on whether there might be any truth to it. If so, we have further investigation to do.

Be willing to lead with your strengths—not your persona.

Lead with Your Strengths

I had an employee who began her career on a relatively narrow track. She had aspirations to do more than her experience qualified her for, which is usually a major barrier, but she had two things working in her favor. First, she possessed clarity about what she wanted to experience, and second, she had great learning agility. She was also passionate and driven about her desired experience, which inspired me as a leader to help her realize that desire. A position in her chosen field came up, and she asked if she could apply for it. Of course I said yes—this was a job I believed would make good use of her detail orientation, her talent for organization and execution, and her love for product.

She interviewed with several people and did not get the job. She was really disappointed. I followed up with some of the folks who interviewed her to get their feedback, and I encouraged her to do the same. What they played back to me was mostly positive, but there were two areas of concern. First, and most obvious, she had no experience in this field. We knew that. Second? When asked for her developmental area or where she sometimes stumbled, she told them she was loud. *Loud?* They interpreted this to mean that she was pushy, bossy, obnoxious, and potentially difficult. I was unpleasantly surprised that with all the skill, talent, and drive this person had, she chose to tell them she was loud. She had come to identify with this personality trait—and not in a good way.

Personal brands in corporate America are good. Labels, however, are not. I had a direct conversation with her about why losing that label was paramount to her own self-definition as well as to how others would perceive her. She understood, and in typical agile fashion, quickly corrected. Only a couple of months later, we were able to secure for her a rotational opportunity in her desired role, where she kicked butt and took names. She is now legitimately serving in that role and doing a great job. She has found her niche and receives glowing feedback for her contributions. To underscore the point, her success has nothing to do with being quiet!

Don't Give Up Your Seat

In my mid-twenties, I was blessed to get my most life-altering work assignment. Hallmark created a product line that featured Dr. Maya Angelou's unique perspective and writings. I was tapped to serve as her editor and the line's editorial director. The work itself held many lessons, but just being around Dr. Angelou was a joy I will never forget. I partnered with her to determine which sentiments we could use and to refine the work to make the best product possible. When I started writing this book, she was still with us. Now that she's passed, it's bittersweet to reflect on the many times I spoke with her, broke bread with her, and learned from her. While I'm sad to know those days are behind me, I'm grateful to have experienced them.

Early in our partnership, my team and I traveled to California for a meeting with Dr. Angelou. There were several others on their way to join us. We were seated at a long rectangular table, and I was directly across from her, engaging in casual conversation. When our guests walked into the room, I stood up to welcome them and casually offered one of the gentlemen my seat. Dr. Angelou started shaking her head at me, telling me "no." I didn't know what was happening at first, but eventually I figured out that she was motioning for me to sit back down. When I did, she leaned in and spoke to me with words and in a tone I will never forget. "You don't have to give up your seat to anyone. You are just as worthy of that seat as he is, and you have every right to sit proudly in it."

In that moment, she was my mirror. She sought to remind me of my inherent value and challenged me to claim my space as a woman— as a Black woman—in that room, in that meeting, in that experience. That stuck with me. Since then, I've continued to ask others to help me see beyond myself, to fortify me, and to inform me of my blind spots, so I can address them and be more of the leader I desire to be. We all need that kind of reminder. And I strive to do that for others.

Mentor 3: The Advocate, or Sponsor

A mentor is someone who advises you, informs you, listens to you, challenges you, and generally supports your growth. A sponsor's commitment to you goes beyond what a mentor does. Sponsorship represents active engagement in identifying opportunities for you, removing barriers, marshaling resources, and creating buy-in with other top leaders who should make your ascent that much smoother.

Sometimes you have sponsors you don't even know about—people who work behind the scenes as your fans and who seek every opportunity to put your name in the hat for visibility, promotion, and recognition.

In 2014, I had the pleasure of speaking at NAFE's In It to Win It leadership conference for female executives. Of the many stimulating conversations we had throughout the day, one that really resonated with me was about whether (and how) women help each other succeed in the workplace. We talked a great deal about mentors versus sponsors, when to seek support, and how to ready yourself for the next level by being clear about what you want to do, why you want to do it, and how you are uniquely skilled to contribute. I found myself nodding my head through most of this ongoing dialogue. There were countless insightful comments made, and I agreed with most of what was shared. But this notion of whether women adequately support each other at work left me a bit restless, and it took me a while to shake it.

I don't know about you, but most (if not all) of my breakthrough opportunities were thoughtfully orchestrated by leaders—those who stepped up to advocate for me. As a side note, they weren't all women, and the role of men as sponsors can't be underestimated. They still hold much of the power in the business world, so it stands to reason that without their genuine support, we will continue to struggle to get ahead. That said, as a female who is acutely aware of the unique complexities inherent in our climbs, I feel strongly that it's not only my responsibility but my privilege to help other women thrive at work.

Because Hallmark is in the relationship business, it's not surprising that we enjoy a disproportionate number of women in leadership positions. This makes our culture very supportive for the most part, but I'm increasingly conscious of the role I should play in raising my own "sister's keeper" high bar. I often wonder how we can help talented, intelligent, passionate women chart their course through what can seem like an unknowable maze of choices and opportunities. For these bright women, succeeding at work shouldn't feel like a labyrinth. And if we want more balanced decision-making at the top, those of us who can help open doors should be more than happy to hang proverbial traffic signs on the walls whenever we can.

In addition to the important role executive women can play in supporting emerging leaders with personal accountability, each of us must ensure we are worthy of a sponsor. That day in Minneapolis, the panel of four successful women from some of the world's best companies shared simple but profound insights. I've captured their guidance for you.

- Focus on consistently strong performance. Strive to be excellent in all things, at all times.

- Take full advantage of springboard moments. Recognize when a presentation, a project, or a simple assignment can provide the treasured opportunity to demonstrate your leadership in profound ways to people who need to know you. Take no chances. Swing for the fences.

- Know and represent yourself well. Per Betty Spence, President of NAFE, you should be able to convey your vision, your professional aspirations, and your differentiated value in two minutes. (By now, you have this down, right?)

- Raise your hand. Is there a special initiative under way? An employee resource group (ERG) leadership position available? A business problem that needs to be solved but hasn't been owned yet? The best way to reach the top is to lead your way there—before you're even asked.

I know some women have had negative experiences with women leaders. One young professional at the conference asked why established women leaders are so threatened by emerging women leaders in the workplace. She went on to explain that she's received more support from men than women, and her experiences left her with a definite impression of the risks and benefits of reliance on one or the other.

I realize this dynamic still exists. Many women have unfortunate stories of being sabotaged by other women, ignored by them, and generally undermined. I'm sure this is even truer in some industries than others, depending on how competitive the environment. Some women still subscribe to the notion that there are only so many spots for women at the top, which can create undesirable behavior on all sides.

While nonsupport from other women is real and can wreak havoc on our confidence in one another, there are increasingly more women who are ready and willing to help others along. The ones who aren't should be seen as individuals who have other priorities, rather than symbols of systemic nonsupport. Believing other women don't want to help you can be more unhelpful than the unhelpful women themselves! Focusing on this belief will isolate you, and prevent you from forming relationships with people who can nurture you, guide you, and stand up for you when the time is right.

Mentor 4: The Gap Filler

The Gap Filler is also known as the antagonist or devil's advocate. This mentor can help you check your assumptions, poke holes in your arguments, and tell you what other people think but won't say about your ideas, your leadership, and your results. This person differs from a mirror mentor in that she or he has little to no interest in whether you become a more reflective and self-aware human being. This person cares about the work and will tell you, without emotion, what she or he really thinks about it. Though this can be a challenging person for you, it's important to understand this counter view.

Accept Tough Feedback

Talking about the Gap Filler makes me think of a story. It was my team's turn to pitch an idea during our monthly product review forum comprised of more than fifty of Hallmark's top executives. We presented our work, shared the good and bad of what we'd learned so far, and opened the floor for feedback to help us strengthen our proposition.

One of the senior executives known for his candor started asking pointed questions about the work, such as how we landed on the assortment, why we chose the technology we did, and how people would understand the idea at shelf. He essentially told us that he didn't buy what we were selling, and did so in an extremely direct way, pulling absolutely no punches.

I listened patiently, asked questions in return where I needed more clarity, respectfully disagreed where appropriate, acknowledged his point when I thought it was valid, and, ultimately, thanked him for his honesty. Here's the thing—he was smart, experienced, and influential. Ignoring his feedback, however harsh, or shifting into a defensive position, wasn't going to further my agenda (which was the work). Even if we had been able to bypass his buy-in for that moment, refusing to address his concerns would have come back to bite us later in the game. To me, there was nothing personal about his questions and commentary. Was it passionate? Yes. Was it tactful? Not especially. Was it valuable? Absolutely.

The most interesting part of this story was what happened in the days following this encounter. People who were there approached me in the halls to ask if I was okay. Some of the words they used to describe his communication toward me? Rude. Disrespectful. Uncalled for. Awkward. Uncomfortable. Even mean. I actually didn't know how to respond. I didn't feel offended, but after listening to everyone's characterization of the interaction, it made me wonder if I should have been. In fact, one of my peers, a matter-of-fact guy, stopped me the next day to ask if the guy who had grilled me sent me flowers. Ha! The unintended benefit for me was a growing reputation for composure. That wasn't my intent. My aim was to be open enough to hear new information that might enhance our work. I have come to know firsthand that personalizing this kind of provocation is the fastest way to shut down conversation and ensure you arrive at a weaker outcome. Make room in your mind for the idea that conflict can be good—and that critical feedback is usually not about you.

To further emphasize the importance of the Gap Filler, I feel absolutely comfortable sharing that the antagonist was right about our idea.

Your Turn

How do you find the right people to support your career goals?

Peer Mentor: You are looking for someone trustworthy, well connected, objective, and seasoned—someone who has been in the organization for five or more years. These qualities ensure that the insights you receive will be fair and informed, and allow you to ask questions in a safe space. Think of three candidates who fit this description and write their names here:

1. _____

2. _____

3. _____

Mirror Mentor: You need someone insightful, thoughtful, respectful, and comfortable negotiating conflict. You want to feel comfortable around this person. It's not easy to convey information people might not want to hear, but your mirror mentor has to be really good at it if you are to receive real value from this relationship. This person doesn't have to work in the same company in order to perceive ways you can get better.

Name three candidates who fit this description:

1. _____

2. _____

3. _____

Advocate: You want someone influential who believes in you and your talents. This someone has the respect of other leaders in decision-making roles. There are often leaders who are beloved by their reports but, for whatever reason, don't necessarily influence the thinking or behavior of their peers. A leader like this is amazing if you want tips on how to become more trusted, but as your advocate? Not the best option.

List three names that come to mind.

1. _____

2. _____

3. _____

Gap Filler: You can ask someone outright to be your devil's advocate. If you choose to go this route, seek someone who is notorious for telling it like it is, and get ready to thicken your skin. It's best if you have a connection with this person, because it makes giving and receiving tough feedback easier on both parties. If you choose not to ask someone specific, you can achieve a similar outcome by asking people in meetings to test your work and requesting timely feedback on your performance or ideas.

Know anyone like this? Write down his or her name.

1. _____

2. _____

3. _____

Now give yourself no more than three months to ask someone from each list to mentor you. Do it in person, and be prepared to explain exactly what kind of mentorship you want.

10

Get in Touch with Your Vulnerability

*E*very leader—no matter how strong or influential—has a story filled with triumphs *and* trials, faith *and* fears, wins *and* losses. We are all flawed, and not only is our humanity normal, there is power in it. People always want to hear success stories. But I believe they need to hear our stories of overcoming challenges too.

Acknowledging your vulnerability doesn't undermine your power, but being ashamed of it sure can. What's more, your ability to truthfully navigate the ups and downs of your career gives others the courage and confidence to know that they, too, can be genuine and successful at the same time. Every misstep has the potential to bring you closer to your desired destination. As long as you look for the lesson in each experience, you will get better. And better. And better.

Accept Your Humanness

Lisa did not come to vulnerability easily. Growing up, she was the classic "good girl." A self-described teacher's pet, she was incredibly smart and a little bossy (today, we call that exhibiting leadership potential), and she prided herself on having all the answers. As a middle child and desperately wanted daughter, she felt she had a lot to live up to, and she worked hard to exceed others' expectations.

As it often does, Lisa's good-girl persona worked well for her throughout her childhood and early adult years. Her drive for perfection was frequently (if not always) rewarded, she earned stellar grades, and the leadership positions she pursued generally came to her. To put it simply, if Lisa played, she generally won. It was this consistent and long-standing pattern of winning that led Lisa to confuse exuding confidence with having confidence, and showing strength with actually being strong.

Lisa entered the workforce in the early 1980s, a time when women were expected to conceal their femininity in order to be taken seriously. The conservative, boxy suits and button-down shirts she wore to fit in were complemented by a direct, ambivalent interpersonal style. Unconsciously, this "good girl" was transformed by a competitive business culture into something of a "good man." At first, this wasn't an issue for Lisa. In fact, she had always seen attributes like empathy and leaning on intuition as signs of weakness. Lisa had modeled herself after her father her entire life. He was strong and confident. Alternatively, she saw her traditional mother as soft and deferent.

Lisa's tough shell started to crack when, after a promotion to a senior product-and-marketing role at Hallmark, she was told that her results were admirable, but her leadership style needed work. When she read the words "You must say 'I don't know' more often" written in black and white on her performance review, she was taken aback. Despite her strong results, Lisa was being mandated, in clear terms, to show more uncertainty. To acknowledge that she didn't have all the answers. To leave space for others to partner with her. And to work harder to build trust. This was an overt signal that the definition of effective leadership was changing from the stereotypically male model of strength, competence, and confidence to something more nuanced.

Upon reflection, Lisa realized she'd experienced this idea years earlier, when she was a marketing manager at a global toy company. Her boss there was a good corporate soldier. He consistently endorsed decisions from on high—even when it was clear those decisions contradicted his values. His team knew things weren't right and they believed he knew it too. They followed his lead but with growing mistrust. If he could confidently advocate for a direction that contradicted his own beliefs, what else was he being dishonest about? Lisa had wished he would be more forthcoming, more willing to share his uncertainty about the direction being given. In her mind, a more authentic approach would have been to say, "I'm not sure this is the answer, but we're going to do it, and we'll learn from it." If he'd been more transparent—more vulnerable—his team would have doubled their efforts to help him win.

Most successful leading women can recall the specific experience or experiences that accelerated their paths to authentic leadership. One of Lisa's watershed moments came when, in conjunction with a challenging new role in Hallmark Retail, she elected to consult with an executive coach. Too often, she was finding herself on the defensive. In one coaching session, the executive coach said something to her she's never forgotten. "*Everyone* has to use *everything* they have."

The coach explained to Lisa that tapping into her insights, her vision, and her empathy—all aspects of her womanhood—was the only way to realize her full potential as a leader. Lisa knew that using her toughness as a shield had put her at professional risk. The time had long since passed for stereotypical male styles of leadership. For the first time, she understood that using her femininity was not the same as using her sexuality. And she realized that if she allowed herself to be caring and empathetic, she wasn't being inappropriate. Instead, she was leveraging her inherent leadership capabilities to get the job done. By integrating all of her capabilities, bringing her whole and authentic self to leadership, she could be more effective, even transformative.

Using everything we have includes taking full advantage of our brain wiring, our nurturing instincts, and even a more self-expressive way of dressing. Lisa began testing her revised leadership approach and found her colleagues extremely receptive. Her peers told her she was less buttoned-up, controlled, and controlling. Her team said they trusted her more, which made them more open to her and her ideas. Everyone with whom she worked now felt more comfortable around Lisa, and it significantly increased her influence in the organization.

These experiences convinced Lisa of the concrete business benefits of being vulnerable. The simple lesson? People want to work with people they feel they know. Lisa believes the only way to truly unleash our organizations' potential—given the volatility, uncertainty, complexity, and ambiguity (V.U.C.A.) around us—is to be willing to show caring and vulnerability to one another and to the people we serve.

In other words, we must become familiar with each other in order to build trust. Trust is the foundation of every healthy debate, courageous risk, and worthwhile negotiation. Without it, people focus on protecting themselves and preserving norms. Leaders today have to enable true and meaningful change, and as women, we must proudly recognize that we are built for just that.

As women, whose unique brand of leadership is needed more than ever, we should embrace the fact that we can wield deep knowledge *and* be deeply known. It's a powerful combination—one Lisa has come to not only embrace but be embraced *for*.

As human beings, we avoid the unknown, and we work hard to shield ourselves from potential ridicule. We do everything we can to make sure others don't find out about our weaknesses—as if they would be surprised to know we have some! In so doing, we limit our ability to get better. The only way for light to shine on a dim area is to expose it, sometimes if only for yourself. Obviously, trust plays a significant role in how comfortable we are being vulnerable at work. Granting trust to others—believing they will respond in a helpful way as opposed to a hurtful way—can feel like an obstacle course in its own right. And there are certainly times when we have to be discerning about exactly what we share and with whom. But living on the guarded end of the spectrum in a work environment that thrives on experimentation and collaboration can be as damaging as trusting the wrong person with too much information. Withholding can isolate you and stunt your professional growth. Don't deny that you have warts. People probably know about them anyway. Instead, own up to them and get the additional support you need to overcome them.

Step Out on a Limb

When I was a creative director, I was asked to participate in a major innovation initiative. A few leaders were chosen to work with a consulting company to learn and adapt a new innovation process and develop several insight-based consumer platforms. Cross-functional teams were created, and I was placed on a team with a product manager and a creative engineer. Since my background was in consumer understanding, creative writing, and editorial strategy, I figured these were the skills required for this work. I quickly realized, however, that I wasn't on the team as a word person. I was on the team as a strategic thinker and problem solver, and our collective charge was to cross the functional boundaries as needed to create the best possible solutions. I was really excited about the opportunity. Boundaries have never really been my thing, so knowing we were not only free to, but encouraged to engage across disciplines was inspiring. That remained true until the team started working on financials. Every time the dollars-and-cents conversation began, I would announce, "Y'all know I don't do numbers." And sometimes, I would actually leave the room. In time, my team members stopped inviting me to financial sessions. I made my limitations clear, and they now believed what I taught them about myself. In a way, I was okay with that. It felt safer.

Making an announcement about my skill gap meant a few things. First, no one could discover that the English major was weak in financial acumen. (I said it first!) Second, I didn't have to experience the discomfort of not getting it in front of people. I took pride in my agility—in my reputation for being sharp and knowledgeable. Honestly, I couldn't bear the thought of struggling to understand something in such a public way. Third and most unfortunately, it meant I robbed myself of a major learning opportunity—almost.

Thankfully, one of the consultants—a man I had great respect for and who was truly invested in my success—pulled me into a conference room one day and asked, "Why do you keep telling people you don't do numbers?" I was caught off guard. I gave him a lame excuse about it not being my thing and how I had other skills I brought to the table. I could have saved my breath. He basically told me that my behavior was unacceptable. He said that if I wanted to do more in the organization— to lead at a higher level and continue to grow—I would have to do numbers. Then he helped me realize that I happened to be in the ideal learning environment. He ordered me back into the room to figure it out with my team.

I was embarrassed, because I knew I was operating in fear. Humbling myself to learn about financials required admitting what I didn't know, so others could deliberately teach me. I've had many more opportunities to use my newfound vulnerability card. When I left the creative division to become a business leader, I used that card fifty ways to Sunday. It is a well-worn card now, and my skill set has broadened considerably as a result.

Get Back Up Again

Vulnerability and the strength born from it aren't always related to work. Because we are human beings first, the challenges—even tragedies—we experience in our personal lives have a dramatic affect on our professional lives too. When faced with the unthinkable, we have less patience for the typical peaks and valleys associated with work. The good news is that we can use these experiences to strengthen our resolve, increase our empathy for others, and focus on what really matters—all of which support a purposeful career.

I have a sister-friend who has been in my life since we were college roommates during our freshman year at Spelman College.

We shared a tight, air condition-less room in an old, brick building that teemed with goal-oriented Black women who would become my lifelong friends. Joslyn Jackson and I graduated from Spelman in 1996 as members of the "Olympic class," a term our then-sister President Johnetta B. Cole affectionately coined to mark a special moment in time. Like college friends do, we graduated and went about the business of living, but we stay in touch and visit when we can.

Joslyn is now a municipal court judge in Atlanta. Due to the anxiety that naturally arises when she walks into a courtroom, she strives to balance her professionalism and authority with a healthy dose of humanity. Joslyn is inherently relatable, a trait that somewhat defines her overall personality. She credits her woman-ness, mother-ness, and daughter-ness for shaping her into the leader she is today, but she acknowledges the many women who have inspired her. While their positional authority may have initially drawn her to them, it was a willingness to share their stories of perseverance that fortified Joslyn over the years, and she is keenly aware of her opportunity to give the same gift to others.

Defendants and visitors often ask to speak to Joslyn at the conclusion of a hearing. She always says yes, even when these conversations follow pretty strict sentences and verbal correction. She believes that every interaction is a possible turning point. For a woman leader who sees her position as an opportunity to positively influence others, these moments are far too valuable to pass up. People usually inquire about Joslyn's career. Young girls who dream of practicing law share their personal challenges or ask whether there's any advice she can give them. Her answer is always the same. "Set a goal and don't stop until you get there," she says. "You are guaranteed to face obstacles so fierce you will question your choices. At times you will run. Other times you will crawl. And sometimes, it will feel like you're scooting mere centimeters at a time. But you must keep moving." Now and then, Joslyn is compelled to share her own personal story of vulnerability turned to strength.

In 2007 Joslyn went back to school to study law. A former banker and owner of a mortgage company, she always had a penchant for getting straight to the heart of the matter. She is a clear thinker and communicator, and she has never shied away from a good debate. When she told me her plans to become an attorney, I wasn't surprised. No one who knows her would be. When Joslyn entered law school, she and her husband had three daughters. They found out they were having a fourth in 2008. As a wife, pregnant mother, and an aspiring lawyer, Joslyn had a hectic life, for sure. But it was about to become much more trying, for her and everyone who loved her.

During Joslyn's second trimester, her obstetrician discovered that the baby inside her had pulmonary valve stenosis—an abnormal development of the heart—as well as underdeveloped kidneys. Joslyn and her husband were concerned, of course. For them, though, there was never a question as to whether she would carry the baby to term. Her pregnancy was relatively uneventful until her last trimester, when Toni Camille was born five weeks early at five pounds. Unsure as to whether the baby could withstand the stress of delivery, Joslyn and her family were exceedingly grateful when this day came. Toni was indeed frail. Her tiny body was overwhelmed with tubes and machines. And still, she was a quintessential Jackson girl—beautiful brown skin, perfectly chiseled features, and a full head of soft, curly hair. Joslyn knew Toni was in a fragile state. The Jackson family and surrounding village prayed for her health to be restored. Her condition grew worse, however, and everyone's greatest fear was realized when she passed away after only seven weeks and five days of life.

Not three days after the Jackson family laid Toni Camille to sleep forever, Joslyn went back to class. Her reentry was with the most dreaded professor in the law school. He was respected for his undeniable knowledge but feared for his artful use of the Socratic method. All students studied extensively before entering his classroom for fear of being embarrassed in front of their colleagues. All summer Joslyn had managed to be well prepared. But not today.

She entered the classroom and sat in the back row. Those who knew her well expressed their condolences amid awkward moments of silence and hugs. There were smiles from across the room from those who didn't know her personally but were aware of what she was going through. She felt uncomfortable and vulnerable in the most extreme sense. But Joslyn believed that class was exactly where she needed to be at that time.

Her professor walked in and, without greeting his class, began to recap the lesson from the week before. Until that day, Joslyn would answer his questions confidently and argue her point, right or wrong. "Fake it 'til you make it" was her strategy, and it had worked well for her. That day, though, her composure was nowhere to be found. Her inside voice begged, "Please don't call on me—please." But within seconds of the thought crossing her mind, he met her gaze. "Ms. Jackson, I see you hiding back there." To this day, Joslyn can't recall the question he asked, but she responded quietly, "I'm not hiding."

"What's that, you say?" he replied. He thought she was just another nervous student coming undone at his critical tone. He had no idea what she had been through. She wanted to scream about how inconsiderate he was, but she didn't. She couldn't. Instead, she whispered to a classmate in front of her, "I can't do this with him today," and hoped the woman would speak up on her behalf. The woman didn't say anything.

With no shield to hide behind, Joslyn stood up from her seat and walked out, leaving her classmates in a state of silent shock. As soon as the door closed behind her, she leaned against the wall and slid to the floor in tears. She could hear the professor resume teaching on the other side of the door, while she sat in a heap trying to pull herself together. He was conducting business as usual. In that moment, reality set in. Joslyn realized that the world around her would indeed go on. Tomorrow would come. And the day after that. Whether or not she was ready, life would continue. And it did.

Eleven months later, Joslyn gave birth to a baby boy, their first son and their daughters' only brother. She is now the sole proprietor of Better Business with Joslyn Jackson, a boutique law firm she created in Atlanta to help clients establish and manage both the legal and financial aspects of small-business ownership. She has a busy and vibrant life, has kept her sense of humor intact, and is more in tune with her strength and courage than ever. Joslyn is a business owner, attorney, judge, wife, daughter, friend, and mother of five children—one of whom taught her more about herself than she ever thought possible.

Joslyn's story is certainly more personal in nature than the others I've included in this book. But I firmly believe that while we can expect colleagues, managers, and employees to be professional, we cannot expect them to be inhuman. Life takes its toll sometimes. And whether we like it or not, our personal tragedies have an impact on how we show up at work. As leaders and especially as women leaders, we have the opportunity to model empathy and compassion for others: To show women what it looks like to acknowledge our vulnerability, while gaining strength from the lessons we've learned. To reference Lisa's story, people want to work for leaders they feel they know and can trust. This is not about broadcasting your personal life. It's about being human and drawing on what is common to all of us.

Your Turn

Did you see yourself in any of these stories? When has vulnerability been a good thing in your career? What makes you afraid of being vulnerable with your colleagues?

Which experiences did they bring to mind that helped you clarify your professional purpose? What lessons did you learn? How have you changed as a result?

I am more_____.

I am less_____.

And lastly, how can you tap into these experiences to further your vision?

11

Go to Happy Hour

Successful businesses thrive on relationships—relationships between ideas, goals, strategies, and, yes, people. It's important to go to happy hour, the company holiday party, the occasional community-service opportunity, or even lunch when you'd rather be working or catching up on emails.

Reaching out to people you don't know is tough for many women and for women of color in particular. We don't like to be "fake." We believe if we show up and work hard, we should get promoted. We believe this, because we're smart and we do a really good job.

But advancement doesn't work that way. Developing trusting relationships puts you in the consideration set. Relationships ensure that people talk *to* you and not *about* you. When there's an issue, relationships invite you to be part of the solution, instead of assuming you're part of the problem. If no one knows you, be prepared to hang out exactly where you are. You will be the best (enter your position here) your company ever had, because you will have many years to master that role and a chance to teach other people who might eventually pass you by. In other words, to move up, you have to put yourself out there.

Make Yourself Known

A few years into her career, Tamara's division reorganized. Some individual contributors were promoted to middle managers, and several other roles were realigned. She was an individual contributor at the time, and people were being notified of their new responsibilities in phases. After a couple months of watching her peers get promoted, she wondered why no one had called her to a higher level of leadership. She was a hard worker. She was smart and talented, and she believed that those with whom she worked closely thought the same.

As each phase of announcements rolled out, she grew more and more confused about the exclusion. After some head-scratching, she decided to ask her manager why she hadn't been considered. The answer? "Nobody knows you." Basically, Tamara had been brought forward as a candidate, and no other decision-makers in the room could vouch for her. It's not that they didn't believe her manager, but Tamara was an unknown entity to them. And people can't advocate with integrity for someone they don't know.

It's what I've come to recognize as the shoulder shrug. There are a bunch of talent managers in a room talking about their employees, and a person's name comes up. Everyone but the person's manager shrugs their shoulders. It's the body-language equivalent of "don't know, won't comment."

When your boss is the only person who can represent your value, you will stagnate. It honestly doesn't matter how brilliant you are. The further you grow in your career, the less likely it is that executives will take one person's opinion as proof that you should be a next-level leader. They will instead believe that you may be really great at your job, but if you were *that* good a leader, they would know you, right? They would have heard about you—news of something you did or said would have gotten to them. Or you, being the leader you are, would have taken initiative to make yourself known.

Of course, superiors aren't the only people worthy of your time and energy. If they think the world of you, but your peers don't trust you, you're in trouble. If subordinates don't want to work for you, well, that's problematic too. Building relationships in corporate America is par for the course. Familiarity breeds trust. Trust is the foundation of collaboration. And since no woman is an island, collaboration is essential.

As you can imagine, Tamara wasted no time pulling herself out of her hard-working hole and went about the business of knowing others and being known. Turns out, her work *and* her life were enriched by the choice. Don't make the mistake of thinking hard work alone will grow your career. It only gets you so far. To reach the top of your game, you need to be connected.

Your Turn

Think of the leaders above you and around you. Do they know who you are? Do they know anything substantive about you? Your goals? Your skills? Your experience?

Here are a few ways to make yourself known:
- Ask your manager if you can present an idea or project at one of their leadership staff meetings. Go prepared to engage the audience in a thoughtful discussion on the topic.

- Set up coffee meetings. Some executives are reluctant to accept lunch meetings, because they use this time to catch up and an hour can feel like a long time for an introductory conversation.

- Get involved in a work-related extracurricular activity with leaders, like a volunteer project or sports event. This gives you a chance to connect in a more natural context.

- Seek opportunities to travel with leaders. There's nothing like a good business trip to create bonds between people who would otherwise not interact.

Your goal is to make connections, and provide a personal and informed point of reference for leaders when your name comes up. While you want to be genuine and careful in your approach, you can't become known without some degree of personal risk.

12

Take on More Work

*P*eople don't get promoted for doing their jobs really well. They get promoted by demonstrating their potential to do more. And that usually happens in the space that goes above and beyond.

I am suggesting in all seriousness that you say yes to more work. More work can come in the form of a special project, leadership of a resource group, participation on an internal team, or just additional responsibilities. Typically, we don't like to give work more time or attention than absolutely necessary. But then we're surprised when work doesn't give us anything back other than what's absolutely required.

To be clear, what is absolutely required is a paycheck. You get hijacked, because you process data better than anyone else. Or you project manage better than anyone else. Or you sell products better than anyone else. All of that may be true. But if that's all you're doing, guess what?

You're doing your job. You are doing your job *really* well. And you are guaranteed to get the awesome opportunity to keep doing your job.

Unfortunately, getting that promotion by taking on more work can take longer than you hope. The waiting game is especially hard when you are busting your tail for an extended period of time to show how worthy you are of next-level leadership. Advancement can only happen when talent and need come together at the same time. Executive leaders can find themselves nurturing talent for months or years, waiting for the right opportunity to take full advantage of a person's strengths and lean into their interests and passions as well. And there's always the question of whether the opportunity will continue to build on her experiences, or if it's just more of the same.

You may have heard it said in spiritual circles that God wants you to wait on Him, but He also cares about how you wait. When it comes to being patient for a promotion, is there a right way to wait? Only you can declare what's right or wrong for you, but there is certainly a way to wait that demonstrates more readiness than you may realize.

Take Jenni, for instance. She spent the first part of her career focusing on completing her tasks well and being a great partner. By the time she began working for Sara, she admitted she hadn't yet given enough energy to career planning. She wanted help positioning herself as the leader she knew she could be, and she was willing to go above and beyond to shift others' perceptions of her from "great team player" to "strategic leader." She never said these things outright, but Sara could tell that by the time Jenni became vocal about advancing, she already had pent-up energy behind the desire. Years of working hard without a declared path to growth had made her somewhat of a teakettle about to reach a boiling point. Sara knew this. But here's the beauty—Jenni didn't behave that way.

Sara told Jenni that shifting others' perceptions of her would require that she be placed on visible assignments with inherent complexity. Other leaders would need to see her think critically, be strategic, manage conflict, and communicate effectively. Honestly, raising her profile wasn't even completely contingent on whether she solved whatever problem Sara threw at her. It was about demonstrating to Sara and others that she could effectively assess a situation, determine the right course of action, and skillfully manage the team, negotiations, and communication. Sara needed to challenge Jenni in enough leadership arenas that others could authentically represent her readiness to advance. After several months, she had become more known to leadership in a good way. She was ready, or at least enough people thought so.

The good thing about taking on more work to demonstrate readiness is that when you're ready, you're ready! There's a feeling of accomplishment in knowing you took full advantage of the opportunity to show and prove, and it's a wonderful feeling. The bad thing? When you're ready, well, you're ready. As in tomorrow. And because the right opportunity isn't always available tomorrow, you can be ready for *months*.

Jenni had a good idea of what kind of work she wanted to do. A few promotional opportunities arose, and she applied for them. More than once, she made it to the final round only to discover that she came in second. Jenni was growing frustrated, and Sara was concerned that she would disengage and lose the passion, energy, and drive that made her such a valuable partner. As her unofficial sponsor, Sara continued to advocate for her to other leaders, while encouraging her to be patient and trust that the right thing would come at the right time. I'm sure Jenni had difficult moments. It would only make sense that she be frustrated after her years of service and commitment to results.

But she didn't show it. She stayed in the game. She kept a smile on her face, continued to collaborate, and volunteered to help others. She made herself available to leaders and peers as a source of knowledge and experience, and she furthered her reputation as someone others could rely on—but now with an added layer of leadership credibility. One year later, Jenni was tapped for a promotion that was tailor-made for her. It combined her passion, experience, knowledge, and even existing relationships into one role—the one she really wanted all along but one that someone else had been in. Sara was really proud of Jenni. Not because she waited—although patience is indeed a virtue. But because of how she waited—professionally, generously, and consistently committed to excellence.

If I haven't convinced you yet, here's what you stand to gain by taking on more work:

1. Visibility

Taking on more work means more people come to understand and value what you have to offer. When you liberally share your expertise, without being overly concerned about what you'll get in return, you'll become known as a helper. Everybody needs help. If you keep doing good work for and with others, people naturally will talk about it. And before you know it, they'll be looking for you—in a good way!

2. Perspective

Working beyond your current assignment gives you an opportunity to see business issues more holistically. One thing I always hear middle managers discuss is how they don't understand why senior managers are making certain decisions. The right thing to do often feels a lot clearer when your scope is smaller, and the information you have is focused on a specific function or goal. Once you rise to a higher level in an organization and you can see the treetops, you realize that what the forest needs may be different than the needs of individual trees. You realize multiple goals exist, and they often conflict. Developing an appreciation for this complexity helps you speak more intelligently about business issues and refines your critical-thinking skills.

3. Skills

What happens when you intentionally seek opportunities to do more? Well, you find them. There are plenty of people, organizations, and communities that can benefit from what you know and what you can do. When you start sharing your experience with others, you automatically refine your skill set. This is because you're exercising those skills in new forums and you're using them more often. It's just like the fundamental workout principle—when you use your muscles often and in new ways, they'll get stronger. The same is true of your skills.

4. Allies

We need each other. Engaging in additional opportunities exposes you to new people and creates authentic connections that enhance both your personal life and your professional life. I've met some amazing people over the years. Each new relationship has opened yet another door. I am exceedingly grateful for those I've met who are making me smarter and more inspired with every interaction. Relationships truly are everything. Give more than is expected, and you will get all kinds of wonder in return.

Welcome Stretch Assignments

Have you ever been offered an opportunity you didn't feel 100 percent prepared for? If not, you should be concerned, and you should immediately seek out that stretch move, or assignment. The stretch move offers a good 70 percent overlap with your skills, talents and passions, and about 30 percent "I have no idea what I'm doing." If you aren't having this kind of experience at least every three years, via a new role or project, you may be stagnating. It can be scary to leap into the stretch move, but I've found that it's more risky to remain status quo. There is not a more compelling way to learn new skills and discover what you're really made of than engaging in a brand-new opportunity. This is where your mentors come into play—to get you *to* the stretch and get you *through* the stretch!

Go Beyond Your Comfort Zone

It was the job of Cherie's dreams. After deciding to leave the workforce to start a family, she was grateful to be back. Making the choice to take a break in a career can be easy for some women and not so much for others. For Cherie, it was a no-brainer. She felt it was imperative that she be fully present for her children in their earliest years. However, after seven precious years at home, she began to feel there was something missing, something more she should be doing. She missed the challenges her former job presented, the relationships she developed with colleagues, and the tasks she completed every day.

She knew it was time for her to go back to work. But knowing it and actually getting the job are two different things. It wasn't easy.

Her résumé was beautifully crafted, but the rather large gap in full-time employment raised eyebrows in the human resources departments where she submitted it. After multiple interviews and some creative follow-up, one media company took a chance on Cherie, marking the beginning of an amazing journey in the second half of her career.

From day one, the job felt perfect. It was fun and creative, the people were welcoming, and Cherie truly felt like she was exactly where she was supposed to be. After one year, she was promoted to the top position in the editorial department. "This is it! It can't get better than this," she thought. Cherie was performing well and gaining recognition throughout the company. Then, two years in, her boss called her into his office.

"I'm resigning, and I think they're going to ask you to take my place," Cherie's boss said. A flood of emotions swept over her, from sadness to uncertainty to a slight twinge of excitement. She went home that day, hopeful, thoughts racing about how, if given the opportunity, she could shape her team to be the best the company had ever seen. But then her inner critic showed up. We all know her—that doubtful, fearful woman who waits in the wings and, when good things appear, comes out and rains on your parade.

"What the heck am I thinking?" Cherie's inner voice challenged her. "I've never managed this many people before. I can't manage a budget that size. Why does my boss have to quit? I like being in the background. I can't do this!" Even after all she accomplished during her time at the company, she still had doubts. For weeks, Cherie went back and forth on what to do, prayed, consulted family and friends, and finally came to a decision. Despite being extremely comfortable in her role in the shadow of her boss, Cherie knew in her heart that she had to accept the job if it was presented to her. It was time to step up to the plate and take on the role as leader of the company's digital department.

Weeks later, when Cherie's boss made his exit, the offer was indeed put on the table. But it wasn't quite what she envisioned. The new responsibilities were there, but the money wasn't—not even close. Devastated and now totally unmotivated, Cherie felt defeated and undervalued. In a welcome shift of perspective, Cherie realized that money didn't have to be her sole motivator. She asked herself how she could turn this into something positive. Could she find the silver lining in all of this?

As part of her negotiations, Cherie carved out a new role and title that would benefit her next career move. Then she took the promotion and set records for her department. She also developed relationships with executives internally and externally in a variety of industries. Most importantly, she gained valuable management and technical skills that she carried with her after leaving the company to start her own digital-strategy enterprise. She learned, as everyone who welcomes the stretch move will, not to be afraid to step out of your comfort zone, even if a new opportunity doesn't look exactly as you thought it would. It could be just what you need to propel you to the next level. Eventually, the new, expanded zone will become comfortable, and you will have to step out again. Each time, you'll be less nervous about it.

Your Turn

Have you ever said no to an assignment because it didn't look like you thought it would?

Have you let self-doubt prevent you from leaping into the professional unknown?

If you happen to be staring at a stretch move, write down the *worst* things that could possibly happen if you go for it. Now write down the *best* things that could possibly happen.

Which list is more compelling? Are you willing to take the risk for the potential benefits?

If so, welcome the stretch move. Say yes, and figure it out as you go.

SECTION 4

SAY YES
TO
THE FUTURE

What would you say if I asked you to shelve every idea you've ever had about what you cannot do? About who won't support you? How you can't break through certain barriers? Why being your whole self at work will never fly?

In order to truly transform your career experience or simply to expand your sphere of influence, you will need a willing suspension of disbelief. You must make room for new ideas, not only about those with whom you work, but also about yourself. Saying yes to the future is another way of saying no to the past, if that past happens to be weighing you down. Clear your mind. It's a new day. Or at least it can be. The choice is yours!

13

Be Open to a New Story

$\mathcal{N}$ews flash—you don't have to wear a mask to be successful. You don't have to be someone you're not. You don't have to play a game. The only way to truly succeed in a way that feels like success on the inside as opposed to sacrifice is to be you. Many of us tell ourselves elaborate stories about why we're not having the experience we desire. And I believe we have to reimagine those stories if we want to live up to our full potential.

Before I start a firestorm here, I'm not suggesting you're imagining things. Many times our stories are based on facts. But just because a story is true doesn't mean it's useful. Please accept this mental reality—whatever story you tell yourself will shape your future. If your story is that it doesn't matter how good you are, you'll never get ahead because you are (female, Black, intimidating, quiet, so-and-so doesn't like you, etc.), you will live that story. If you decide it's important to be right, you'll keep telling that story to yourself and others, and you'll get stuck.

On the other hand, if you decide it's more important to be effective, you will ask questions, seek clarification about what others perceive (versus what you interpret), and make it your business to craft a new story—one that aligns with the experience you want to have. You will look for signs of progress, not signs of defeat. And those signs will multiply. Don't hide behind your beliefs about what other people think about you. Know who you are. And consistently be the best you possible, in every circumstance.

Be Careful What You Believe

Carol, a first-level manager at a consulting firm, wanted a promotion to senior manager and needed to demonstrate her leadership potential. She believed the only way she could showcase her ability to win new business, build an effective team, and brilliantly deliver was to move to a new account and serve as lead project manager. Instead, her advisors encouraged her to take advantage of a step-up opportunity as a team member of an existing account in order to be perceived as next-level material. Unfortunately, that's not what Carol

" The only way to truly succeed in a way that feels like success on the inside as opposed to sacrifice is to be you. "

had in mind. Meanwhile, she continued to serve as a valuable member of her team for several months.

At her annual review, she learned she would not be promoted, because she hadn't demonstrated leadership in her current role. Carol desired to be seen as a subject-matter expert, which meant training the next set of leaders and developing consistent models of delivery. While she participated in best-practice sessions, built tools and templates, and created and ran estimation models, she fell short of suggesting ways to replicate these models for broader use. She neglected to make good on an opportunity to effectively launch an ERG—a clear leadership platform that was handed to her on a silver platter.

In short, Carol hadn't made it a priority to understand what next-level leadership looked like, to clarify and socialize her differentiated value, or to advocate for herself. Doing any of these things would have increased her chances of advancing. She was unable to take advantage of an opportunity staring her in the face, because she was convinced she had to be the boss in order to lead.

Leadership isn't about being the boss. It's about identifying needs and filling them. Instead of doing that, Carol was waiting for a position to which she felt entitled. Her story suddenly included that she was passed over. She wasn't provided the chance to lead, and it was because she was African American—and no one on her team was looking out for her. Instead of using the constructive feedback she had received to shape her next steps, she resisted it and added it to her story that there was something wrong with her managers, because they just didn't recognize her skills.

As the blame cycle goes, it was everyone else's fault that Carol didn't get promoted. A year later, she left the company to take a first-level manager position somewhere else. Is it possible that some aspects of her story are true? Sure. But her story wasn't helpful to her. Instead, she could have been the leader she believed she was, regardless of her title. She could have risen to the occasion, solved problems, helped develop others, and brought her ideas to the table. What's the lesson? The best way to demonstrate your value is to be excellent—*from where you are.* Then you have a much better shot at moving onward and upward.

Our words have power, and so do our thoughts. Everything we do originates with a thought. And so it stands to reason that guarding our thoughts and choosing them carefully is of utmost importance if we want to live our best lives.

Debra McDermed, who presented the concept of self-generative energy to our team at Hallmark, also introduced us to the thought cycle over ten years ago during a creative leadership session. While the concept has been espoused everywhere, from the Bible to the school system, bringing it into the workplace was a revolutionary idea at the time. We learned to see how our thoughts contributed to our experiences. All these years later, I am highly conscious of the many counterproductive stories that get told and retold along cultural lines, and the role they play in stagnating one's professional journey.

Choose Your Thoughts Wisely

"I have to be twice as good as anyone else to succeed."

"It's not what you know, it's who you know."

"It doesn't matter how hard I work. I'll always get overlooked."

"People like me aren't seen as leadership material."

Do any of these statements sound familiar? Have you told yourself any of these stories about your advancement opportunities, others' perceptions of you, or your company's leadership? If the answer is yes, I'm asking you—lovingly and respectfully—to stop.

Hang in there with me. I'm not asking you to stop because I don't believe these dynamics exist. I know they do. Unconscious bias is real in the workplace, and anyone who claims otherwise is either not being honest or not paying attention. So these and other statements like them may very well be true. But here's the thing— they're not helpful. What do I mean by that? We know that any thought we think often enough becomes a belief. Our beliefs about ourselves, our circumstances, and those with whom we interact cause emotional reactions. Our emotions influence our behaviors. And our behaviors often dictate—or at least heavily influence—our results. If Proverbs 23:7 is true, that "as a man [or woman] thinketh in his heart, so is he [or she]," then you can see how repeatedly telling yourself a story like the examples above can guarantee an experience much like the one you wish to avoid.

I've mentored many people over the years, and I've watched enough people travel diverse career paths to know that the link between our thoughts and our outcomes cannot be denied or underestimated.

So how does this work, practically speaking?

- **Belief:** It doesn't matter how hard I work, I'll always get overlooked.

- **Emotions:** Hopeless, resentful.

- **Behaviors:** Isolate yourself. Keep your head down. Perhaps work hard but with limited passion or energy. (Because it won't matter anyway.)

- **Result:** You aren't identified for promotional opportunities or high-profile assignments—not because you're not smart or capable—because leaders may not know you or understand your value, and because you demonstrate a perceived (or real) lack of passion or energy when leadership agility is at a premium.

The reason I want us to stop telling these negative stories is because they nullify our power. We all have creative power. If you can think a counterproductive thought so many times that it changes how you show up, then you can think a productive one. And that, too, will change how you show up.

I encourage women to deeply explore the concept of changing one's thoughts, because I've found that many of us aren't even aware of the role we play in our own career experiences. And if we are aware, we may wonder what we're doing wrong, but we don't ask how we may be "thinking wrong." We often fail to assess our self-talk and the impact it can have on our day-to-day experiences. We oversimplify. We believe what we see. But what happens when what we see is a direct result of the lens through which we are viewing the situation?

There's a pretty simple process you can use to explore the story you're living and, more importantly, to consciously live a new one.

- Where is your greatest pain point at work? Why do you believe it's painful? Who is involved? What do you think about the people involved? What do you believe they're motivated by? What do you believe they think about you?

- What evidence do you have that your beliefs or thoughts are true? What has happened to confirm your beliefs? Could there be another explanation? Have any events contradicted your beliefs? Is your evidence true? How do you know?

- What would happen if you flipped your thoughts about the situation? Is there a scenario where you could abandon the negative belief in favor of a possibility-driven one? Would anything bad happen if you dropped the negative thoughts? If you think, for instance, that someone doesn't want to help you, what would happen if you instead think they *do*? Would you do anything differently?

- What do you *prefer* to be experiencing relative to this situation? How do you want to feel? What kind of result are you hoping for?

- What are three things you might do to get closer to your desired experience?

Decide today to put a new thought into your own personal thought cycle. Tell yourself a hopeful story about your future possibilities—one you can get excited about. Commit to it the way you may have committed to some other, less-helpful belief. Become conscious of the way this new story makes you feel, and give yourself permission to believe it long enough to experience the surprises that occur as a result. You can do it—if you think you can.

14

Achieve a New Level
of Leadership

*I*f you've been reading this book in order, you now have most of
what you need to develop a strategy for advancing your professional
purpose. You've identified your beliefs and values, the reason you work,
your differentiated value, your skill gaps, and a few targeted ways
you can fill those gaps. You've read about various support structures
and the importance of extending yourself. You've even explored your
own thoughts about your career. I hope you've committed to getting
your mind right about your future. You are more than able to achieve
anything you set your mind to, if you do the work on you and approach
your potential with optimism. Being a great leader is absolutely in your
reach. But is there more than greatness? Is there an even higher level of

leadership that takes you beyond success and effectiveness to something lasting—memorable, even?

If I consult my heart on the matter, which I often do, I boil this down to a simple concept: A memorable leader's contributions keep working long after she stops working. I've thought about this a lot lately, mostly because my leadership philosophy has been inspired by women whose legacies continue to inspire me, years after I worked with them or for them. Although they've moved on to other adventures, their lessons live on. Here are a few of the traits that make them great.

1. Purpose

Transformational leaders have a clear and passionate purpose. They desire to leave people and situations better than they found them. Every day, while crunching numbers or setting strategies, they believe they're contributing to something more meaningful than the day's task list. Hard work may happen in the valley, but true change takes place on that higher ground we explored in the first section of the book.

2. Humanity

Call it authenticity, empathy, emotional intelligence, or compassion. The most memorable leaders are real. They're genuine. They not only *think* their way through business challenges, they *feel* their way through them. These leaders are consistent, create a safe environment in which to take risks, and aren't afraid to lean into their beliefs and values when warranted. Memorable leaders remember that we are human beings, not humans doing.

3. Agility

Ever work with someone who set a direction and refused to change it, even when every signal suggested he or she should? You can call it persistence or focus or discipline. But you can't call it agile. Agile leaders are in tune with their surroundings. They are hyperconscious of the benefits and risks associated with their decisions and make adjustments as new information becomes available. They're not afraid to be labeled "wishy-washy"—when the situation changes, so do they. Quickly.

4. Courage

Unforgettable leaders say the hard stuff. They ask tough questions, make tough decisions, and tenaciously contend with tough issues without fear of retribution. They encourage honesty and model it for others. Memorable leaders know the truth is always best—even if others aren't quite ready to hear it. Great leaders go where others won't and effectively take people along with them.

5. Confidence

Memorable leaders believe in themselves. They know the value they bring to the party and represent it with equal parts passion and poise. They believe in their ability to change things for the better, and they flawlessly collaborate with others in the name of progress. Their confidence makes their team confident—in their leadership, yes, but also in their members' own leadership. Associate with people who believe in themselves and in your inherent value. It's contagious. In a good way.

Develop Emotional Intelligence

When I first told my friend Teresa that I was writing a leadership book, she asked if I knew Jo Miller, CEO of Women's Leadership Coaching and founding editor of *Be Leaderly*. I knew of Jo, but I hadn't heard her speak or read her work.

When I got home that night, I sent Jo an invitation to connect online and began following her blogs. I would tag her in my posts now and then, and she would kindly respond. Several weeks later, we learned we'd be speaking at the same conference. She sent me a note suggesting we connect in the hotel lobby the night I arrived, since she had to leave early the next morning to catch a flight. I arrived after 10 p.m., Jo rode the elevator down to meet me, and we talked for a brief but memorable fifteen minutes. The day she told me the below story, I confessed to her that her desire to meet *me* was an incredible and inspiring surprise. I didn't realize that our brief encounter would be just the beginning of a friendship.

Jo was born in South Australia and attended the University of Adelaide. Her first foray into the workforce after graduation was exciting by any definition. She started working for a small, vibrant freelance agency for the publishing and advertising industries, and Jo managed the creative staff. Armed with fresh business knowledge and ready to take on the world, she began her new adventure. What she quickly learned, however, was that her new opportunity was less about running a business and more about people management. The company was created from her manager's network, whose entire career was built on the foundation of these relationships. It was a professional and personal treasure of sorts. On its face, the focus on people sounds like a nonissue. And it would have been, except that Jo claims she lacked the skills we've all come to know as critical to successful leadership—social and emotional intelligence.

Knowing Jo today, it's hard to believe she ever operated this way. But as she explains it, her analytical mind just didn't think about this sort of thing. It wasn't long before her skill gap began causing problems for Jo and the business partners for whom she worked. Managing people is difficult, but managing creative people is something else entirely.

Jo's leader sat her down and asked what it would take to bring her out of her shell. This wasn't the first time someone had asked Jo a question like this, but she truly didn't get it. It just wasn't apparent to her that emotional intelligence was "a thing." She didn't easily open up to others, she had a difficult time with social intimacy, and she wasn't building the trust necessary to get the most from her team.

Jo took a few personal and professional-development classes that her managers recommended, and she found them challenging in some ways. But overall, she didn't like being under the microscope. One day, she became so upset with one of the business partners that Jo called her a "bitch." Shortly thereafter, Jo got fired. This unfortunate event coincided with the breakup of a five-year relationship. It was definitely a tough time for her. She had entered the workforce full of enthusiasm, but she quickly crashed and burned.

Jo decided to relocate to a new city and start again. A friend suggested she read *Emotional Intelligence* by Daniel Goleman. She chuckles as she recounts having to read it a couple times before it sunk in, but she admits it dramatically changed her approach to everything.

Jo began thinking (analytically, of course!) about how to further develop her emotional intelligence. Who were the people she admired? She paid attention to how they interacted with others, their manner of speech, and how they mentored and built relationships. She wrote a checklist of behaviors she wanted to emulate, and she lined up a coach to help her along the way. Jo set a goal to have as much executive presence as her model leader. With time and practice, Jo lost the fear of being around people and of speaking up, which she acknowledges comprised her shell in the first place.

Jo knew she had made progress when, during a phone call, her client said, "You sound different today." Jo joked that someone put Prozac in her coffee, and the laughter came easily. Her confidence had arrived. Her mojo was working. Today, Jo is a keynote speaker and advises women and companies on a range of topics intended to strengthen women's leadership skills and inspire them to take the reigns. She suggests identifying a few role models and deconstructing their approaches—not to be like them, but to follow their guidelines for effectiveness. After all, doing so worked for her.

There are many ways to be a great leader, but becoming a memorable one requires tapping into your very core—knowing not only what you're working on, but also who you are, and what you're working for. Memorable leaders work from deep roots. If you haven't already, I encourage you to find yours.

Your Turn

- Which traits in this chapter resonate most?

- Do these traits ring true when you think about leaders you deem unforgettable? Can you think of examples?

- When you receive feedback about your leadership, do any of the themes mentioned show up? Which ones?

- What ways can you further leverage the memorable traits that come most naturally to you? Can you consciously own them? (They will make the difference!)

15

Discover a New Opportunity

Sometimes, no matter how hard you try, how well you network, how many opportunities you take on to stretch yourself and grow, things just don't work. There is no wisdom in remaining in a misaligned situation for an extended period of time. When your talents and skills don't match the job you are being asked to do, you will not succeed—not because you failed or "just couldn't figure it out," but because you and your role aren't well suited for each other. A bad fit seldom gets better with time. I often tell friends who are in misaligned romantic relationships that a breakup doesn't have to mean one person was bad or didn't try hard enough. There's not always an enemy. It can be that you just don't want the same things. Or that what you each bring as individuals isn't complementary. Or that you just can't "work" together. The same is true of employees and jobs, or companies. Sometimes the best thing you can do for yourself is something else.

Seek the Right Fit

Michelle was beloved in a role she held for a long time. She had experiential knowledge, raw talent, and insights that made her a credible leader in her field. She was also extremely personable and well liked. Michelle left her company for a time and came back in a different role. It was a field she had passion for but not necessarily skills or experience. It was a role that required extensive technical knowledge and also, likely, a different personality than Michelle possessed. She was patient, inclusive, and believed everything would work itself out. She was an optimist by nature. She also was an intelligent woman who knew a lot about a lot of things and was obviously an agile learner. But the complexities inherent in her new role required more than agility—they required a specific type of know-how.

Time revealed that Michelle was not the right person for that particular role. In the course of a few short years, her colleagues saw a beloved leader become what some label a "lame duck." She was perceived as woefully ineffective. And this went on for far too long. It was unfortunate on many fronts. For starters, her company lost valuable time and opportunity during this stretch in an area where they needed to win. And the most unfortunate outcome was a loss of trust in Michelle as a leader.

Fit is everything. I encourage you to be completely aware of the alignment between your skills and your role. And please avoid taking a wildly off-course assignment that is likely to end badly. I've been known to out myself when I'm not in alignment. It's not a popular position. I've had superiors look at me sideways when I have either asked to be taken off the succession list for certain types of roles or expressed the desire to do something different for the good of the work, the team, and my own effectiveness. But awareness is paramount. The goal is not to say yes to anything at any cost—it's to be effective and aligned, so you can be your best self and do your best work.

I know taking the initiative to leave an unpleasant work situation is scary. Many of us live such that our lifestyles and our incomes are interdependent. If one changes, the other must change too. And because we work hard to create stability for our families and ourselves, the thought of shifting from a seemingly sure thing—no matter how miserable we are—to an unsure thing sounds not only difficult but unwise. But advancing your professional purpose is about the long term. I assume you're interested in purpose-driven work or you wouldn't be reading this book. And as with anything worthwhile, we sometimes have to make difficult choices for the greater good. Staying put in a bad fit endangers your emotional well-being, your reputation, your business goals, and those whom you lead. While it can be hard to transition, more is often at risk in not doing so.

Below are a few ways to tell when it's time to explore a new opportunity.

- **Check your gut.** How do you feel when you get up in the morning to go to work? If occasionally you're not feeling it, that's normal. But if it's been weeks to months and every morning you wish you were selling piña coladas in Hawaii, you may be misaligned in your current role. Leading with your strengths creates energy. Having to operate in your skill gap for too long is draining, even for the most responsible workers. Your emotional response to being miscast can range from boredom to constant frustration to anger.

- **Check your results.** Are you delivering against your goals? If so, on a scale of 1 to 10, how easy or difficult has it been for you? Does everything feel like a burden, or is there a balance of struggles and easy wins? If you're not delivering, is it circumstantial? Or is it more like perpetually banging your head against the wall? If it's just too hard, *all the time*, you may be miscast. When you're in a good job fit, it doesn't feel like drudgery, even when the work is truly challenging and the barriers are great.

• **Check your feedback.** If you haven't received unsolicited positive feedback from peers, bosses, or directs in more than six months, that's a signal. If you work in a culture where no one gets unsolicited feedback, then ask your stakeholders for it. Conversely, if you work in a culture where unsolicited positive feedback flows like water, get pointed feedback on your performance. If the responses are minimal or mostly focused on development, you may be miscast.

If you are indeed misaligned, be encouraged. I've heard countless stories from women who found themselves in seemingly impossible situations, only to rise from the ashes, so to speak. A poor job fit isn't the end of the world. In fact, it can be just the beginning.

Declare Your Future Success

Glenda has always been a high achiever. Like many accomplished career women, success came naturally to her, especially during childhood and early adult years. Easy wins can be a good thing, but the downside for Glenda was the boredom that always followed. Whenever she didn't feel appropriately challenged, her engagement suffered.

In college, Glenda was an economics major, and she studied labor statistics and human resources in graduate school. She grew up near Detroit, where the auto industry's value for human-resources expertise shaped her view of the kind of work she might do someday. Because of this influence, she was not only academically trained to be a human-resources professional but environmentally trained as well.

After completing grad school, Glenda began her career as a labor-relations representative for one of the Big Three automotive companies. While she understood human-resources curriculum and laws, the reality of the day-to-day job made her feel like a bit of an anomaly. An innate questioner and process pioneer of sorts, she frequently challenged existing policies, and she was a dissenting voice in many workplace debates. She didn't realize that by speaking her mind and providing her opinion, she was perceived as combative. Glenda was accused of overthinking situations and challenging norms in such a way that made others uncomfortable. Every time she received this feedback, she would grow more frustrated. "Why isn't questioning welcome?" she wondered. The frustration and associated overthinking spun into a cycle from which Glenda couldn't easily extract herself. She felt marginalized and underutilized. Here she was, a young professional with a lot to offer but no clear path by which to offer it.

After a while, Glenda decided she would try harder to fit in and follow the rules. She pacified her true nature by telling herself that not every issue required a response or an opinion, and she began to suppress her ideas to avoid being misunderstood. This approach, though undesirable, seemed to work for a while. Glenda was even promoted to higher levels of leadership. Around this time, Glenda's mother—the primary reason she still called Michigan home—passed away.

Glenda could have stayed with her company, continued to advance, and increased her salary, but money no longer motivated her the way it once had. She wanted more. Glenda opened herself to other opportunities and eventually left Michigan to pursue a job in talent acquisition at a major beverage company in Atlanta. She believed she could be satisfied in this type of role—that making people happy by helping them find employment would in turn make her happy.

Glenda was really good at her new job. She had an eye for talent, and she was adept at connecting great people to positions that best leveraged their skills and interests. But while the role itself had redeeming qualities, it required Glenda to do things she wasn't comfortable doing. For example, she prefers intimate social circles, and the job required a high degree of social interaction, which was uncomfortable at times. The harder she tried to find her happy place, the more frustrated she felt. As many of us have experienced, being in the wrong role teaches us a great deal about whom we are. It also teaches us who we are *not*.

Seven years into her career in Atlanta, the company downsized. As the talent-acquisition lead, Glenda played a prominent role in this change and, as is the norm, human resources was last to be impacted. While her job would not be eliminated, it *would* be downgraded, which meant she had the option to stay and accept the new terms or exit the organization.

Glenda was underwhelmed with the idea of staying put, so she applied for other roles within the company. She summarizes the result of that search as divine intervention. "God has a way of closing every door you think should be propped open in order to guide you where He wants you to go," she explains. Glenda is generally confident, but she remembers this period as the first time in her career that she questioned her abilities. Most people would cling more tightly to the sure thing in a situation like this, but while her colleagues advised her to stay, she didn't want to.

A month later, Glenda made the unpopular decision to leave, joining her husband's company. She wanted to be more strategic, and she saw an opportunity to lend her business-management skills to his operation. She believed their complementary backgrounds would balance each other and enable greater success. One short year after she joined him, however, it became painfully clear she'd made a mistake. They had different philosophies, and were ultimately unable to maintain their marriage and grow the business at the same time. It seemed their entire relationship now revolved around the company. Of course, in typical analytical fashion, Glenda dug in and tried to fix it. Time revealed, however, that neither the company nor the marriage was for her to fix.

Three years after leaving the beverage company, Glenda and her husband divorced. She describes her revelation in basic terms. "I looked up one day, and I had no husband, no business, no job and very little money." Glenda was the consistent financial source in her marriage. Every time the business needed a shot in the arm, she administered it. As a result, she was now deep in debt. There was a point at which she considered going back to a big company. She even applied for jobs beneath her skill level, trying to regain some sense of stability. But again, God closed every door. Glenda was at her lowest, and during this time, she doubted whether she was ever as good as she thought she was. It's difficult to see the big picture when rejection is staring you in the face.

It was in this dark place that Glenda remembered a man with whom she'd partnered in the auto industry. She reached out, telling him that she'd left her last job and planned to start a consulting business in communications and media, an area she'd explored in her previous role. He explained that he was now publisher of a major magazine targeting affluent African-American consumers and celebrating the luxury lifestyle of urban professionals and influencers. It just so happened that this magazine needed help establishing a new professional division, so he invited the CEO to join their phone call and proceeded to explain how Glenda's corporate experience and new company made her the perfect person to help launch their new division. Before the terms were even finalized, Glenda said yes. With one phone call, Glenda's media company was born, and the magazine became her first client.

Public relations and communications offer the right fit for Glenda's personality. She's assertive and enjoys deadline-driven work and project management. She thrives on strategic thinking and planning, and she finds inspiration in helping others achieve their goals. The ability to leverage her platform to elevate others and spread their messages brings her great satisfaction.

Years later, the publisher, who connected Glenda to her first client, left to work for another magazine. The CEO expanded her role, and she assumed responsibility for all corporate editorial content, corporate events, and partnerships as Vice President for Corporate and Strategic Partnerships. At this point, Glenda had spent 18 years in corporate America and no matter how hard she worked, the vice president title had always eluded her—until now. What's more, she hadn't asked for it. It was offered to her based on her commitment, her results, and her differentiated value.

I asked Glenda if she has any advice for women who are seeking a new opportunity. For starters, she strongly suggests maintaining a keen sense of self-awareness, unless you want to find yourself subject to someone else's idea of you. She also warns women against chasing money. Instead, she says, seek a move for the growth, learning, and alignment it provides. She recognizes that it can be challenging to analyze yourself when you're in the valley.

When she shared her story about being at her lowest point, she explained, "My lights had been out! During those times, I would go to the coffee shop, come home at night when it was already dark, and go straight to sleep." Glenda encourages us to stay focused on our vision for our lives. Without realizing how profound a statement it is, she casually ended her valley story with words that brought my own life lessons to mind. "Even in the dark," Glenda emphasized, "I declared what I wanted to experience."

Glenda is now comfortable in her own skin. She has a great career and a renewed life. And seeing how this all happened for her after age forty, she's grateful to know—and wants you to know too—that it's never too late to find your professional home.

16

Embrace a New You

I can't help it. I'm possibility minded. If you've read this far, you're committed to growing your influence and living your professional purpose. And if you're committed, you are able. It's never too late to redefine your career experience. You can do so in the role you're in by applying new strategies. Or you might shift to a different role within the same company. Or you may need to make a more significant change. Whatever your situation, a stronger, more purposeful you is absolutely within your grasp. It doesn't really matter how far you believe you have to travel. What matters is what you're willing to do now. Can you embrace a new, more-optimistic, purpose-filled you?

Be the Woman You Believe In

Yesi Morrillo-Gual is an executive director at one of the world's largest financial institutions. She also founded a personal and professional development network that educates, empowers, and enlightens Latina women to rise to their full potential. Today, a wife and mother of two sons, Yesi—the queen of planning—is earning her fourth degree, enjoys working with women engaged in her network for which she produces an annual conference, offers monthly webinars, hosts networking events and workshops, and maintains an active and engaging social-media presence.

The path to her current reality, however, was paved with hardship. Yesi's parents were born in the Dominican Republic. Her father was a carpenter and her mother was a homemaker. Yesi's father was determined to raise their five children in the United States, where he hoped they would become professionals, and he dedicated his life to ensuring that she and her four brothers would have the best possible chance to succeed. Unfortunately for Yesi and her family, life dealt an unexpected blow.

When Yesi was just five years old, her mother found her father lifeless in bed one morning. He had suffered a heart attack. Things began to unravel for Yesi's family after that. Her mother, who had a second-grade education and spoke no English, mentally checked out, and, ultimately, decided she was not up to the task of raising five children. Yesi and her four siblings were scattered across various cities, and she ended up staying with her mother's uncle in lower Manhattan and then in Boston with a stepsister.

At the tender age of seven, she worked in a supermarket packing bags with groceries for customers. Other jobs she took on to help make ends meet included redeeming bottles. She would go to school during the day and collect bottles for redemption at night when her friends couldn't see her.

Yesi's first inspiration came from books. She recalls reading stories about people with amazing lives and feeling inspired to live the kind of life she had only seen in the pages of books. But friends and family members, young and old, discouraged her, saying she wouldn't amount to anything. This only made Yesi more determined to live the life of her dreams.

Yesi paid her way through Baruch College in New York by typing students' research papers and résumés. After graduation, she landed a position with a financial institution. When she started, she remembers being the only person of color with a strong desire for career advancement. She got married, and two years after she started her career, she gave birth to her first son.

In time, Yesi became the first Latina Executive Director in her division of five hundred people. When her promotion was announced, other people of color found her to say they, too, wanted to excel, but they weren't sure how to break through. She developed a heart for helping others grow professionally, providing insights she had gained along the way.

Interestingly, even as Yesi supported the women in her company, she still lacked her own source of professional strength—a network of women from her background who understood her unique challenges and context. Yesi sought out this network externally, becoming an active member of one such organization. Ultimately, she realized she had the passion and desire to define and grow her own network, and in 2010— fifteen years after she launched her career—she created Proud to Be Latina (PTBL).

PTBL was created to help Latinas banish self-doubt and break self-imposed barriers. The network provides a forum where Latinas can connect, and it offers advancement strategies and knowledge-based programs to help them reach the highest levels of success to make an impact in their organizations and communities. Yesi speaks about how engaged her husband and two sons are in her business, passing out flyers, helping her connect to new members, and preparing for special events. Yesi's professional journey is a family affair, which makes it all the more enriching for her.

Yesi's story is among the strongest examples of creative power I have heard. Step by step, she imagined and manifested the professional experience she desired. She believed not only in herself but in something and someone greater than herself.

Today, Yesi is the woman she believed she could be. While I'm sure there are core attributes of that young girl still at play—curiosity, strong work ethic, courage—she has become the product of her own creative power. She is an inspiring, successful, multifaceted family woman and professional whom others look up to as an example of what's possible. No matter where you are on your professional journey, you too can refine or redefine your career and yourself.

Say Yes: The Final Word

There's nothing more inspiring to me than watching a bright, passionate female leader come into her own. I truly believe the business world needs you now, and I want you to be prepared. I want you to know yourself better than anyone else knows you. I want you to have more than the desire to define your professional destiny—I want you to have the ability to define it. And the confidence to live it!

Many of the concepts explained in this book aren't taught in class. There are personal-brand workshops everywhere, and most companies offer leadership-development training. But for women and women of color in particular, there are unique issues at play. Some of these issues—e.g., lack of robust networks and hesitancy to promote oneself—are rooted in beliefs to which we ourselves cling, even when they hinder our progress. Other issues are rooted in beliefs others have about us. Some are institutional in nature and comprised of decades after decades of systems and processes that have left us out. In my mind, an important first step to leveling the playing field is to raise our collective consciousness about the differentiated value we add to the business world—not despite our femaleness but because of it.

Fitness professionals often talk about the importance of core strength. Strengthening your core includes developing the deep layer of abdominal muscles that do important work for your body. They support your spine to help you stand up straight, and they tighten the adjacent muscles. In essence, core conditioning strengthens your body from the inside out.

The same is true of purpose-driven work. Being fully aware of your core essence is a prerequisite to effectively leveraging your gifts. Once you know who you are, how you want to contribute and how you are uniquely equipped, you can confidently step into your future, with your eyes open and your head held high. You are not alone in this journey. There are women just like you all over the world who desire more from their careers and have found themselves in need, at one time or another, of additional strength.

It's your time. You matter and have incredible gifts to give, just as you are. Be yourself, and bring to your business ventures your stories, your perspectives, your insights, and your ideas. Strive to bring your best to the table at all times, and commit to developing meaningful connections and skills that will help you make your best even better.

What would happen if when you closed this book, you chose to believe that anything is possible for you? Even when the evidence may suggest otherwise? Ultimately, you represent you. Make that important work count. Every day, no matter where I am or what I'm doing, I'll be cheering you on. And waiting with pride and anticipation for the women in leadership trends to change for the better, thanks to you.

Say yes, ladies. To your values. Your talents. Your vision. And your purpose. Say yes to a future rich with possibility, imagined by you and manifested by intention, focus, and a commitment to excellence. You can do this! The business world is waiting.

With love and best wishes,
Tara Jaye

BONUS

A Letter to the Business World

This book is for emerging women leaders and those who are knocking on the door of executive leadership but for whatever reason, they haven't made it inside. That said, there are insights to be gleaned for male and female executives as well. While my purpose is to better prepare women of all backgrounds to confidently lead, I would be remiss if I didn't share—at least at a high level—what business leaders can do to help ensure that their seeds of greatness are planted in fertile ground.

There are wonderful books, articles, and research studies on unconscious bias. We generally understand the concept and the effects of it, and we have identified some ways to combat it. But in the spirit of a practical approach, I'd like to share three things women leaders need from you that you can actually give. You may not be able to single-

171

handedly dismantle a culture of unconscious bias overnight, but as an individual leader, you can commit to consciousness and raise it in others, starting right now.

One of the unfortunate employment trends for women and women of color, in particular, shows that if they rise into leadership

> **You may not be able to single-handedly dismantle a culture of unconscious bias overnight, but as an individual leader, you can commit to consciousness and raise it in others, starting right now.**

at all, they stagnate in middle management. They are considered solid enough performers to be promoted, but they are not seen as worthy of breaking through to the executive level. Why? Many of these women are every bit as capable as those who seemingly fly through the ranks on a magic carpet. In some cases, however, they're not as informed. And they're certainly not as connected. Often, they don't see themselves reflected at the top and aren't sure with whom they can safely connect, so they just hope management will notice how hard they work, how reliable they are, and how badly they want to lead. They keep pushing, waiting to be invited to work on that major project or the next breakthrough idea.

Champions for diversity and inclusion have the power to provide the insights, access, and intervention necessary to clear the way for those who have more to give than their current circumstances allow.

We should be hypervigilant about identifying unique perspectives and differentiated talents that can add value to our teams. Looking out for unique candidates not only serves you but your business goals. Diverse points of view result in a more comprehensive vision.

1. Insight

Every executive leader has been given the skinny by someone who went before. There are always cultural norms, unwritten rules, and insider knowledge about the company's most valuable leadership traits or sacred cows. Some professionals and especially culturally diverse professionals often find themselves outside of this insight loop. That means you have to pull them into that loop, on purpose. Do you intentionally and freely share what you know about the business and its strategy? Do you connect aspiring culturally diverse women leaders to people they should know, and who should know them? When we generously share our insights, connections are made, and mutual benefits are born.

2. Access

As we've discussed, one of the best ways to get experiential learning is through involvement in cross-divisional projects, leadership programs, or other high-visibility initiatives. This is one place where employees who fall outside of the cultural norms tend to miss out on the action. Middle and senior managers usually have their go-to team. These folks become known as versatile, responsive, strategic players who jump into ambiguous situations and make good things happen. What we fail to appreciate is that they become high performers in part because they're talented, but also thanks to the opportunities they've been given. (Insert the crazy-making phrase, "I just want the best person for the job"—the best people are the best because others invest in them.) There are many people in our companies who have never been chosen for these stretch opportunities, but who—with experience and exposure—could be just as powerful as the next person. We have to provide access consciously. Equally. And often. Goodness knows there's enough important work to go around.

3. Intervention

Every well-established company has processes, policies, and systems by which people advance. These systems are so ingrained and consistently applied that we develop shortcuts by which to execute them. How do we streamline? What can we assume and therefore not spend too much time discussing? If we are to ensure all employees get enough airtime, we need to interrupt our normal course of business and ask different questions. Add new people to the list. Reach down deeper into the organization than the top ten who are typically discussed. How can you intervene to alter the conversation in your company? The consideration set doesn't change without intent. The only kind of shift that happens in these situations is a deliberate one.

Inclusive organizations are healthier, creative, and drive stronger results. I write this not as a diversity and inclusion practitioner, but as a business leader. If we hope to fully harness the performance power of an inclusive workforce, we've got to get better at pulling people up through the middle. There isn't one glass ceiling, there are several. And while we may not have the power to single-handedly break them all, there are some in our very own houses that we can and should do something about. The world is changing so fast, and especially now, we need conscious leadership of all kinds.

More about "The Best Person for the Job"

Whenever I talk or write about this topic, someone will inevitably say, "I don't believe in spending extra effort developing or seeking out any one group—we hire the best person for the job." I understand this response on the surface, but it completely ignores the fact that employees become the best person for the job over time and because of their experiences. Depending on the business climate and diversity awareness, many women and people of color don't get the benefit of these experiences.

I write about insight, access, and intervention to counteract this trend. We must get out of autopilot on this one. Many executives believe that their good intentions are enough to change the women in leadership trends that have been stagnant for years. Your good intentions are wonderful. But they're insufficient. You have to understand that there are, in fact, gender and cultural differences at play that make it more challenging for women and people of color to traverse work cultures that were built by and for white men. This is not a complaint or an excuse. It's a fact. For women and people of color, some corporate cultures are the equivalent of an American competing with Brazilians in an Amazonian scavenger hunt. At the risk of oversimplifying, that American is going to have some disadvantages.

I know some still perceive diversity/inclusion as no more than politically correct discourse. Others see it as the right thing to do. In my opinion, this is not the most important reason you should care about it. I still hear many business leaders grasping for proof that diversity drives business results. Honestly, I don't blame them for grasping. Sure, some people ask because they don't really believe it impacts the bottom line.

But others ask because they do believe, and they're looking for more data points to help others believe along with them.

Inclusion is undoubtedly a business issue, and while I could cite examples of how diverse teams drove improved business performance, I'm not going to. The Internet offers countless examples, and I won't spend time on that here. Instead, I'd like to share five commonsense but underappreciated consequences of a homogeneous workforce. If nothing else, I hope you can appreciate the power of perception, insight, and trends at play in these examples, and the fact that their impact will increase in presence and influence over time.

1. Scary Blind Spots

Anyone remember the 2011 Nivea ad for shaving cream that suggested Blacks needed to re-civilize themselves? The print ad showed a well-dressed, clean-shaven Black man tossing the head of a not-so clean-shaven Afro-wearing male like a bowling ball. The print ad stated "Look like you give a damn." I'm betting neither the advertising team nor the brand team had a Black person on it, or this would have never made it past concept stage. We all make mistakes, but with a diverse team, some mistakes are avoidable.

2. Limp Leadership Commitment

Employees pay attention to the people who receive promotions. Essentially, they're looking for reflections of themselves as a way to gauge their own advancement potential. If a young working mother sees no working moms at high levels of the company, she doesn't believe she can be a mom *and* an executive. If you have no gay execs or no one is "out" at work, a gay man doesn't believe he can succeed *and* bring his whole self to work. It seems obvious, but a lack of diversity at the top can compromise engagement in the middle. People believe they will only go so far, which makes them subconsciously temper their contributions. The risk is similar to giving your heart to a partner you don't believe will ever marry you. It's not a great investment.

3. Confidence Issues

You want to serve the needs of a multicultural America? So does every company with one eye on population growth and the other on the rich well of insight from consumers whose values are aspirational for the total market. A homogenous workforce has to rely heavily on research and a handful of diverse employees for understanding and translation. Without sufficient diversity in decision-making roles, leaders will naturally—and smartly—check and double-check their assumptions. Intuitive or in-culture knowledge at all levels of the company is faster and cheaper, and it builds on itself. When your leaders have inherent understanding of diverse markets, they make calls more confidently.

4. Ugly Prom Date

Millennials don't see diversity as an initiative. For them, it's a way of life. They all—white and nonwhite—grew up in a world rich with ideas and diverse perspectives, and they prefer the same in a workplace. Price Waterhouse Cooper released a study in 2013 called "Next Generation Diversity: Developing Tomorrow's Female Leaders." In this report, they cite that the millennial generation tends to seek employers with a strong record on equality and diversity. In particular, this is important to the female millennial. A total of 82% identify an employer's policy on diversity, equality, and workforce inclusion as important when deciding whether to work for an organization.

5. You Can't Play

Perhaps the most significant, albeit emerging, risk of a lack of workforce diversity is the growing expectation that a company's workforce should reflect its consumers. From legal to marketing to retailing, the question is being asked of vendors and suppliers more often, and those who don't make the cut can be excluded from the consideration set. An astute businesswoman I know likened it to the conversation about environmentalism. At first, reducing your business's carbon footprint was a nice-to-have characteristic. It differentiated leading businesses from those that weren't engaged. Over time, it became a requirement. The companies who didn't "get straight in line" were eventually kicked out of the line altogether.

Data that proves inclusion drives business results is important, but it doesn't tell the whole story. The benefits of a diverse workforce go well beyond what we can quantify through a register or on a P&L report. We can't forget the opportunity cost associated with not having a diverse workforce, which is always harder to pin down. Trust that it matters. It does. And work with your leaders to chart a path to tangible progress, sooner rather than later. Fortunately and unfortunately, the "nice-to-have" clock is running out.

ACKNOWLEDGEMENTS

I wrote *Say Yes* to pay homage to the women (and men!) who have made me the leader I am today. These include Paul Barker, Eileen Drummond, Lois Hunt, Teri Ann Drake, Ellen Junger, Kim Newton, and Pete Burney. I feel blessed to have worked for and with people who know their self-worth, consistently model courageous and authentic leadership, and embrace me for who I am. They provided insights and advocacy, and they took the time to understand what I had to offer. Then they intentionally placed me in situations where I could offer it. Every female leader should be so fortunate. I'm not saying this as a flippant expression. I literally mean *every* female leader *should* be this fortunate, and if she's not, there's work to be done not only by that leader, but also by her manager, and often the company for which she works.

I also wrote this book because I felt compelled to. I've seen firsthand the good things that happen when leaders from different perspectives come together in the name of business results. Innovation and engagement are both tied to diversity in the broadest sense. I've also watched women struggle to find their footing and to carve out their space in the hierarchy. Over the years, I've coached as many women as I possibly could. Seeing as how my time and opportunities are limited, I felt that writing *Say Yes* was the best way to extend not only the lessons I've learned and taught over the years, but the love and encouragement I've received and given as well. The push and the support. We all need them, but we don't all get them.

Thanks be to God. This book has been a long time coming. I want to acknowledge David Taylor and Teresa Olsen, my catalysts;

Teresa's dad, John Garrity, who taught me the basics of long-form writing; and John Glynn, who gave me the title for this book after listening to me ramble for an hour about my experiences. Thanks to Erica Keith for her visual magic; Samuel Jordan Jr., Royal Photography, for making me look good; and Jacquelyn Fletcher and Karin Miller for their editing brilliance. Thanks to my parents, John and Marlene Centeio, for always encouraging my creativity and reminding me of the strength in my Cape Verdean roots; my children for inspiring me and forgiving my late-night writing sessions; and my husband, John, for being my hero and always standing in the gap for me. I married up!

A heartfelt and tearful thank you to Jen Seyller and Lindsey Roy Eusterwiemann. Without them, I wouldn't be where I am right now. To my many sister-friends, especially Brenda Scott, Melissa McKenzie, and Kim Preston, who literally and figuratively carried me through my personal trials—I cherish you. I also want to thank the women who told me their personal stories and added dimension to the principles in this book, and the kind leaders who endorsed *Say Yes*, especially Don Hall Jr., whose vision and leadership continue to make me proud to be a Hallmarker. Lastly, thanks to Jacquelyn Fletcher, my publisher, who took a chance—and a leap of faith—with me. And thanks to Maggie Knoke, who introduced me to Jacquelyn. I am eternally grateful.

ABOUT THE AUTHOR

Tara Jaye Frank, Vice President of Multicultural Strategy for Hallmark Cards, Inc., is responsible for partnering across product development, marketing, and retail to drive growth with an increasingly diverse consumer base. She leads the company's newly established multicultural center of excellence, whose work has inspired a more holistic approach to leveraging the nuance of culture as a foundational and innovative path to relevance.

Tara began her Hallmark career as a greeting-card writer in 1996 and has held both creative and business-leadership positions. She was the youngest person in Hallmark's history to be promoted into executive management. Subsequently, she became its first African-American female vice president.

Over a decade of leadership coaching has made Tara a known source of guidance and inspiration for leaders who aspire to create professional visions they can believe in and achieve. She passionately guides people toward recognizing their own professional power as well as the inherent value in others.

Tara has spoken across the country on leadership topics, such as Emotional Intelligence, The Power of Belief, and Practical Visioning and Planning.

Tara holds a bachelor's degree in English from Spelman College in Atlanta. She's a member of Delta Sigma Theta Sorority, Inc., and she is a published children's book author. She lives in Dallas, Texas, with her husband John, five of their six children—ages eight to eighteen—and their two dogs.

Get in touch at Tarajayefrank.com or @tarajfrank.